CAN'T STOP WALKING

CAN'T STOP WALKING

*Every Walk Must First Begin with a Step,
Purpose, and Direction*

MURPHY V. S. ANDERSON
Foreword by Eric M. Allison

RESOURCE *Publications* • Eugene, Oregon

CAN'T STOP WALKING
Every Walk Must First Begin with a Step, Purpose, and Direction

Copyright © 2021 Murphy V. S. Anderson. All rights reserved. Except for brief quotations in critical publications or reviews, no part of this book may be reproduced in any manner without prior written permission from the publisher. Write: Permissions, Wipf and Stock Publishers, 199 W. 8th Ave., Suite 3, Eugene, OR 97401.

Limit of Liability/Disclaimer of Warranty: The author has used his best judgments and efforts in preparing this book. Therefore, he makes no representations or warranties concerning the accuracy or completeness of this book's content. He specifically disclaims any implied warranties of merchantability or fitness for a particular purpose. No warranty may be created or extended by sales representatives or written sales materials. The strategies used by the characters in this book may not be suitable or applicable in your situation. Therefore, the author shall not be liable for damages arising here.

The author does not necessarily endorse any organization, warring factions, or websites because of the information gathered from them and/or cited in this book. The author wishes to caution his readers to be aware that some of the websites cited may have been removed, changed, replaced, or no longer exist between when this book was written and finally published.

Resource Publications
An Imprint of Wipf and Stock Publishers
199 W. 8th Ave., Suite 3
Eugene, OR 97401

www.wipfandstock.com

PAPERBACK ISBN: 978-1-7252-9556-8
HARDCOVER ISBN: 978-1-7252-9555-1
EBOOK ISBN: 978-1-7252-9557-5

04/13/21

In loving memory of two soldiers of the faith,
Rev. George Garpue and Rev. G. Nathaniel B. Garpue
(Aka, Uncle Nat)
and
the citizens of Saye Wheh Town

Every walk must begin with a step, purpose, and direction; the dangers ahead of a walk may be avoided by those who circumspectly walk away from them and not those who walk into them.

ANONYMOUS

Contents

Foreword by Eric M. Allison	ix
Preface	xi
Acknowledgments	xv
Chapter One: Unfamiliar Pathways	1
Chapter Two: What Happens When Tradition Clashes with Civility	11
Chapter Three: New Life in a Strange Town	21
Chapter Four: Reshaping the Minds of the Youth amid a Civil War	29
Chapter Five: Gold Mining	44
Chapter Six: Evil in the Heart of a God-Fearing Man	54
Chapter Seven: What Happens When Cultural and Traditional Practices Overrun Spirituality?	71
Chapter Eight: Animal by Night, Human by Day—A Supernatural Encounter	79
Chapter Nine: A Mysterious Birth	90
Chapter Ten: Black Sunday	96
Appendix: Glossary of Traditional Liberian Names and Meanings	117
About the Author	121
Bibliography	123

Foreword

It is a unique opportunity for me to be asked by an aspiring African (Liberian) scholar and author, Murphy V. S. Anderson, to craft this prelude to his new book—*Can't Stop Walking*. This is a sequel to his first masterpiece, titled *A Journey to Bong Mines*.... It would stimulate the curiosity of the reader to know that Murphy happens to be a relative of mine, a maternal cousin. Both of us share a similar worldview as Africans (Liberians) serving God and humanity in this twenty-first-century world.

Can't Stop Walking is the continuing story of four friends who reluctantly escaped a rebel attack on their hometown, set within the context of an African civil war. Determined to get to their destination—the ancestral village of the oldest—they embarked on a long journey, on foot, that took them through bush paths, hills, a forest, several villages, and a river. They finally arrived at their place of refuge, so they thought. While in the ancestral village, each of the four friends (three males and one female) had a challenging experience. Just when they were trying to settle down and started working to help transform the social and spiritual lives of citizens of the town, it came under attack by a rebel commander and his forces. Sadly, they all fled the town and had to travel again, on foot, to a northern city, not far from the borders of a neighboring country. Suspecting a major onslaught on their nation's capital, and after some soul-searching, the four friends finally decided to cross over into the neighboring country, thus becoming refugees. It is my hope that everyone eager to capture a glimpse of an emerging African continent will read this book.

Rev. Dr. Eric M. Allison, DMin, MTh
Pastor, People's Community Evangelical Lutheran Church
Baltimore, Maryland, USA

Preface

A STORY IS TOLD about a young boy who lived with his parents during the civil war between North and South Vietnam in the 1950s. One early morning, his father awoke and told the boy to accompany him to the next town about eighty-five kilometers south of their village to gather rice and other food items because they had run out of food and other basic household goods. The war had driven the family deep into hardship and starvation. Therefore, the realization of death was inevitable if a drastic decision was not made quickly to rescue them.

The boy looked his father in his eyes and said, "Father, I would love to come with you, but the walk to the other town is too far, and the way to get there is risky and unfamiliar to us. I am afraid that we might fall in the hands of the Southern Vietnamese Army and be killed."

His father, who had no options but to risk his life and the life of his only son, told the boy these words: "Every walk must begin with a step, purpose, and direction; the dangers ahead of a walk may be avoided by those who circumspectly walk away from them and not those who walk into them." He looked into his son's eyes and said, "Come and let us go, child, we will hopefully make it there and come back home. God is our protector; he will lead and guide us through this walk and make sure that we come back to your mom and sisters safely."

Walking can be viewed as a form of exercise or physical activity that reinvigorates the energy supply to the human body, especially when done intentionally or purposefully. However, walking may become tiring or burdensome under extreme conditions that a person is compelled to undergo or withstand to survive. Walking at a 3–5 m/h (5–8 km/h) pace expands enough energy to be classified as moderate intensity. It is an easy and accessible way of meeting physical activity recommendations.[1]

Walking may also be considered a mental exercise, not only executed by physical means but also by a mental process. An individual may take a

1. Hanson and Jones, "Is There Evidence."

walk of purpose that is mentally conceived and processed through a journey of life but has no physical bearings, demonstrations, or movements of his or her body. For example, a preacher may deliver a sermon where he or she takes the audience on a journey or a walk through a dispensation, an event in history, or biblical chronology without physically walking through it.

Studies show that walking has immense health benefits and more for the human body when done periodically or constantly. Walking as compared to vigorous exercise is a relatively accessible form of physical activity. It requires less cardiovascular and muscular effort and is less likely to cause serious injury. Walking is also inexpensive and does not require special equipment or facilities. However, walking for physical activity may be hindered by unique factors, such as concern over appearance, sweating, clothing restrictions, uncomfortable shoes, and having to carry other items such as shopping bags or suitcases.[2]

In this book, you will soon realize that the walk being discussed herein is different from an ordinary walk for pleasure, exercise, or health reasons. Instead, it was a compulsory walk initiated primarily for survival and solitude. It was a walk driven by fear of the unknown and the unfolding rivalry between two or more warring factions, which forced the movement of peaceful civilians across Liberia from one city, town, or village to the next.

Can't Stop Walking is a book uniquely written to bring the reader mentally closer to some information that may seem awkward but realistic and true, experiences that may probably be considered inconceivable and trivial but factual. The book reveals the continual and unwavering efforts by Kerkula and his friend Uncle Nat to escape hostilities, the fear of conscription, and bloodshed by moving toward peaceful grounds. It discusses the direct opposite of what it means to wander away from one's hometown into the unknown, a society where there are no parents, siblings, or relatives—a small town located in the heart of a district that has been considered for decades as the "melting pot" of Bong County. This was a result of new outbreaks of hostilities, sufferings, and deaths. The book reveals some of the cultural, societal, and social ways of life of the inhabitants of Saye Wheh Town, a small but unique town situated in the heart of Kokoyah District, Bong County. It divulges the immeasurable power of God to protect those who seek him and call on his name for protection in times of crisis.

In this book, the reader will come to understand the following: What happens when tradition clashes with civility? How does an unprepared person cope with the challenges and difficulties of working in gold mines for the first time? What happens when evil is found in the heart of the one who

2. Dunton and Schneider, "Perceived Barriers to Walking."

professes to be a God-fearing Christian? What happens when leaders of a local church allow tradition and cultural practices to take preeminence and influence its members' spirituality and kingdom-mindedness? How possible is it for a human being to become an "animal" at night and a human by day?

The revelations of these truths are evidence of the power of God to save and protect the innocence of those he loves and cares about from the things hidden and unfamiliar to them. However, the discussions of these truths are in no way an indictment or challenge to any person, groups of people, culture, tradition, community, or society but a means of fulfilling the burden to inform which God has laid on the author's heart. Additionally, the stories contained herein are in no way meant to relive the memories of events that transpired. Neither are they intended to decry, ridicule, or demonize anyone else. The author recognizes that some of his readers may become critical or hypersensitive to the approach he uses in this book. However, the author intends to use any legally recognizable and acceptable platforms to create opportunities for all Liberians to discuss the issues that have impacted us one way or the other as a nation and people. He encourages all Liberians to seek and find similar platforms and utilize the opportunities available to do the same.

This book is mostly based on true stories about the individuals, church, and town. The stories are also true about the individuals who revealed them to the writer. The names mentioned herein have purposely been reduced to initials or first names to protect the individuals' identities, culture, and traditional rites. For the most part, the stories are true to the author's recollections even though it has been several years since the stories were told or occurred.

Though the physical war may have ended in Liberia and life is beginning to return to some levels of normalcy, we will continue to walk mentally until we return to our ancestors' land and play our individual and collective roles as citizens of the republic. In so doing, we would have fulfilled our obligations to all those who came before us.

This book's publication would not have been possible without the gracious friendships and love of the individuals to whom I have dedicated it. Though some of them are no longer with us, their love, ministries, leaderships, and outspoken and fearless dispositions will forever be treasured. The Revs. George and Nathaniel Garpue were brothers and true soldiers of the cross of Christ who understood their calls to ministry. These two individuals had personal relationships with God, evident by their lives, the ministries they were involved with, and the love they demonstrated for their fellow men. They will always be missed!

Acknowledgments

If anyone ever told you writing a book was an easy undertaking, ask them to show you a copy of a book they have written so you can decide for yourself. Whether you choose to believe it or not, writing a book is not as easy as some would like to think. There are many essential elements one must consider in writing a book successfully. However, I would like to think that to write a book successfully, one must either have a story to tell, a clear and vivid imagination or information about an event, an ability to translate the story or information into sensible and readable literature, and most importantly, he or she must have people who can relate to and make sense of the information he or she has written about.

Therefore, I would like to thank the following individuals who helped me make this book project a success. I would like to thank God for the wisdom, knowledge, inspiration, and desire he has given me to write. My heartfelt thanks go to Revs. George and Nathaniel Garpue on whose good works this book has been written. Thanks to Rev. and Mrs. David Tonga for their contributions on names and meanings from Nimba County. Thanks to the Sunnyway family for the information and pictures they shared with me about Saye Wheh Town and Mr. Lincoln Sirleaf, my little Brother in Sanniquelle who helped me to gather pictures from the gold mines in Nimba County. Thanks to Rev. Dr. Eric Allison for writing the foreword and additional contributions to this project. My heartfelt thanks and appreciation go to the citizens of Saye Wheh Town for their indirect contributions to the stories and lessons within this book. I want to thank them for creating opportunities that challenged and impacted my faith and forced me to realize that God is supreme above all other gods. Finally, I would like to thank everyone who helped gather the information needed to complete this book. I am indebted to all of you for your kind assistance and hard work.

CHAPTER ONE

Unfamiliar Pathways

But small is the gate and narrow the road that leads to life, and only a few find it.

—Matthew 7:14 NIV

It was apparent that neither Kerkula, Uncle Nat, or the other two individuals with them knew exactly where they were headed. For a moment, Kerkula seemed bemused and hesitant about walking through the bushy paths which the fighter had instructed them to take. To him, this was unfamiliar territory that he knew nothing about and did not want to travel. He began to reflect on the previous conversation they had with the G-2 officer at the checkpoint, which made him question his kindness toward them.

At one point, he thought to himself, This must be a setup to endanger us. I think the fighter has given us directions that would lead us directly in harm's way, without voicing his opinion to Uncle Nat or the others. He was too skeptical to voice his opinion because he thought they would have ridiculed or laughed at him. He also thought his colleagues would have considered him pessimistic and afraid. Therefore, he kept walking on to the verge of the young bush where the actual walk leading from the checkpoint would have started.

Kerkula was always mindful of being criticized or looked at as being scared or weak-minded by his peers. He always protected his emotions and thoughts but spoke openly when he was convinced without a doubt that his thought process and suggestions would make sense and be accepted by others around him. He was afraid of regrets. Therefore, he made sure not to make decisions or put forward suggestions that could have negative or unsuccessful outcomes. He was inclined to avoid taking an uncalculated risk or making uneducated judgments.

At first, he was under the impression that Uncle Nat was familiar with the terrain. He was convinced Uncle Nat knew exactly how to lead them through the countryside to their destination, considering the level of conversation they had with the G-2 officer and how relaxed he appeared. Soon, he found out that Uncle Nat was in the same boat as everyone else. The difference was that Uncle Nat always kept his cool no matter the circumstance he was in or had encountered. Unlike Kerkula, he was not concerned or troubled by the mistakes he made or being criticized for the decisions he took. He was not ashamed about his personal beliefs, religion, or opinions that he provided on many subjects he had strong convictions about. He was fearlessly confident about what he did, said, and believed.

Uncle Nat took the lead during the walk as he passed Kerkula and the others, singing local gospel songs and some of his favorite hymns. He sang songs like "We've Come This Far by Faith"; "Amongst the Other Gods, You Are Faithful Lord"; "Jehovah Jireh Reigneth, Forever"; and hymns like "How Great Thou Art"; "Old Rugged Cross"; and "Jesus Paid It All." He kept on inviting Kerkula and the others to join him in singing along as he took his time to walk up and down the narrow pathways and in the shades of tall trees. He looked behind constantly to make sure the others were right behind him as he picked up the pace in walking and signing.

Uncle Nat may have been best known for many things; singing was not one of them. He could sing and knew how to lead songs that would meet the musical needs of occasions and events. He helped lead praise and worship at conventions and during Bible studies. He loved to sing and start programs or events when others seemed hesitant to take the lead. He always believed if no one was willing to step up and undertake a task, he would regardless if it were done at perfection or with mistakes.

THE WALK THROUGH THE DARK FOREST

The sun stood overhead above the trees and shined brightly, making the forest clear and easy to navigate. The forest was peaceful and quiet. There was no one else on the roads when the journey started, at least for the first couple of minutes. It was easier to hear birds of different kinds throughout the forest. Some whispered nearby while others squawked and chirped afar in the hills and tall trees. Animals like tree squirrels, deer, and rabbits ran the young forest floor while creeping sounds of insects and the burbling noise of running streams from the hillside and valleys below were heard from the distance as the four individuals sang and walked the unfamiliar pathways.

Villagers going from town to town to conduct trade and commerce and others leaving their farms early in the evening were also seen on the roads further during the journey. Some of the villagers along the roads greeted Kerkula and the others in Kpelle. It was clear they were in Bong County, which is predominantly inhabited by the Kpelle tribe, one of several tribal groups in Liberia. Unfortunately, others did not want to be bothered and careless about exchanging greetings. Some did not want any forms of interaction with strangers along the roads. Interestingly, some were afraid of the unknown; they could not determine who was a fighter or an ordinary civilian since both the fighters and civilians looked and acted almost the same apart from those who wore uniforms, fighter's attire, or carried weapons on them.

It is typically customary in Liberia for villagers walking along pathways to warmly greet each other, especially when it was clear to them that they might be from either the same or nearby villages. This is almost true today, even with the end of the civil crisis three decades ago. Liberians are societal or community-oriented people who love and believe in each other. Unfortunately, they do not support each other as much as they profess to love one another. They are most hospitable to strangers, people from different communities and countries, more than their neighbors or relatives. They are more likely to believe what a stranger has to say or offer them rather than a fellow community member or neighbor. Above all else, Liberians are engaging and can easily be engaged or encouraged to become a part of a process.

As they walked the pathways through the forest, the evening was coming upon them quickly as the bright sunlight slowly dissipated. They came across an older man and his son walking slowly along the paths. They both looked tired but alert. The boy was younger and approximately between the ages of twelve and fifteen years old. They were returning from their farm and probably had fallen behind other farmers who came from the same direction. The older man had a gallon of palm oil and another gallon of bamboo wine in his left hand, a single barrel shotgun on his back with the sling fastened across his chest, and a cutlass in his right hand. The boy was wearing traditionally made shot pants, often referred to in Liberia as boombor. He did not have footwear or a shirt on his back. He struggled to carry a bundle of firewood on his head.

Upon reaching the boy and his father, Uncle Nat greeted them immediately in Bassa, and the older man responded in the same vernacular.

Both men chatted for a couple of minutes while Kerkula and the other two individuals stood by and listened. They were not involved in the conversations because they could not understand or speak Bassa.

Kerkula began to empathize with the little boy who had to carry the big bundle of firewood on his head. Hence, he offered to help carry it for him until they reach his village. He picked up the bundle of firewood and put it on his shoulder and said to the others, "Let's go," but he was still standing in the same position. There is an adage in Liberia that says if you tell someone, "Let us go," you should already be moving or ahead of the person and not standing in the same position. The older man realized that Kerkula did not know about the adage or understand the meaning of it. Therefore, he patted Uncle Nat on his back and asked him to walk along with him. Both men began to walk ahead while the others followed behind. Soon, they reached an intersection after walking approximately twenty-five minutes from where they started.

The old man stopped abruptly in the middle of the road, turned to Uncle Nat, and spoke in Bassa, "We have to leave you now. We are going on this other road to our village." He pointed to a smaller and grassy path that led through a young bush a few yards from the forest where they had walked. He told Uncle Nat, "Continue with this road until you reach the waterside ahead of you where there is a raft that would take you and your friends to the other side of the river. There, you will find people in the town who will direct you on how to get to where you are going. Good luck!" This was the only time the old man spoke English. Uncle Nat, Kerkula, and the other two individuals were shocked when they heard the older man speaking in English.

Though Uncle Nat was pleased with the conversations he had with the old man, he wondered why he chose not to speak in English but Bassa throughout the walk. He later figured out, and revealed to his friends, that a traditionalist, especially an elder, would rather speak in his or her native language instead of English, even if he or she is fluent in speaking English. This is done this way for several reasons. Elders, who are traditionally and culturally minded, would prefer to speak in their native vernaculars for several reasons: 1) to maintain the true meaning and identity of what they are communicating. For example, the use of words to describe a specific person, place, thing, or event; 2) the difficulties experienced when interpreting or translating parables from their native tongues to English. Often, our traditional elders would speak in parables to demonstrate and protect several cultural norms, including teaching lasting lessons to the younger generation or making connections to certain cultural and traditional norms or ancestral beliefs; and 3) to prevent or exclude others from fully participating or understanding what is being discussed in their conversations. Liberia has rich cultures and traditions that encourage or support several traditional societies for both males and females—for example, the Poro and Sande societies. Only members can participate in their activities or be allowed to get involved in their conversations. Members of these traditional societies are mindful of speaking openly about their traditional rituals and practices to non-members or in their presence. It is forbidden for members of traditional societal groups to disobey traditional rituals and practices that are sacred and exclusive to members only. Members who violate such rituals are usually disciplined by the elders or prominent individuals of the society.

Apart from these listed above, there are other reasons to suggest why our elders prefer to speak in their native tongue rather than English. A fourth reason for this preference is the inability of our elders to fluently communicate in English due to the lack of understanding as a result of the high illiteracy rate currently in Liberia.

ILLITERACY IN LIBERIA

Liberia is amongst several third-world or developing nations on the lower levels of the world's literacy scale. According to the United Nations Educational, Scientific and Cultural Organization (UNESCO) statistical reports, 2008 and 2017 respectively, the illiteracy rates for Liberians aged fifteen years were 64.96 percent (males) and 45.64 percent (females); for fifteen years and older they were 62.7 percent (males) and 34.01 percent (females); and for adults aged sixty-five years and older they were 56.85 percent (males) and 12.33 percent (females).[1] This is compared to the global literacy rates of 86.3 percent for ages fifteen years or older, 90 percent (males), and 82.7 percent (females). This means citizens from countries with higher literacy rates, mainly age fifteen years and above, can properly read and write while countries with low literacy rates at ages fifteen years and older cannot. Unfortunately, Liberia is no exception and must take the needed steps to educate its citizens.

Several reasons can be attributed to Liberia's failure to achieve higher literacy rates for its citizens. They include but are not limited to the following.

---

1. "Liberia."

Inadequate Investments in Education

The failures of past and current administrations to adequately invest in different levels of education, especially the education of the younger generation who are the future of the nation, has presented and continues to pose national threats to our existence as a people and country, the economy, human resource development, and Liberia's role in the community of nations.

According to an article carried in *FrontPage Africa* on January 17, 2020, the More4Education Coalition Partners, a conglomerate of civil society organizations in Liberia, expressed deep concerns over the percentage of funding for education in the 2019–2020 fiscal budget. The budget listed only a percentage increase in government funding for education for this period, which increased from 13.7 percent in the 2017–2018 fiscal budget to 14.07 percent in the current budget (2019–2020) compared to Sierra Leone, which invested 27 percent, and Ghana, 35 percent, in 2018 respectively. The article also suggests that comparing Liberia's investment in education to other countries' in the same region shows a disproportionate contribution made by the Liberian government. The article concludes that Liberia is lagging far behind the investment curve in education.[2]

According to the 2018 Final Report by Global Partnership for Education (GPE), the government of Liberia invested approximately $83.8 million in domestic education between 2010 and 2017, which amounted to a 13–15 percent increase. However, funding in education dropped as low as 10.6 percent during 2014–2015 and from 62 percent in 2012/2013 to 52 percent in 2015/2016. Interestingly, donor contributions to education in Liberia between 2001 and 2014 made up 30–50 percent of the total budget.[3]

Failure of Past Administrations to Recognize Education as the Bedrock of National Security and Development.

The refusal by past administrations during the early history of Liberia to invest in education and recognize it as the bedrock of any nation's security and development has contributed to the high rate of illiteracy in Liberia. These are key reasons why the national government does not see the need to invest in education adequately. The priority of past administrations has not been education but self-enrichments. Any Liberian who has reached the age required for voting in a general election has a constitutional obligation to exercise his or her right to vote in removing a sitting administration if his

2. Dunbar, "Liberia: More4Education Coalition."
3. "Summative Evaluation."

or her right to achieving quality education has been violated or suppressed. Unfortunately, the average Liberian nowadays is not concerned about achieving quality education. Instead, he or she is interested in other sectors of the country, like trade and commerce, infrastructure development, and the acquisition of personal wealth, which indicates one of the ways how the government prioritizes and invests funding.

This does not mean that the pursuit of these initiatives by ordinary Liberians is wrong or against the national interest. However, if education is considered the bedrock of any nation or democracy, then the pursuit of quality education must supersede everything else. Education, in every sense, is one of the fundamental pillars of development. No country can achieve sustainable economic growth and development without substantial investment in human capital because education enriches people's understanding of themselves and the world.[4]

Ravi Zacharias, Christian apologist and founder of Ravi Zacharias International Ministries, put it right when he said that the greatest pursuit of the Hebrews was light, the ideal of the Romans was glory, and the Greeks pursued knowledge.[5] Therefore, what can we say is the greatest pursuit of Liberians or Liberia as a country?

Corruption and Poor Governance

You do not need to ask the experts about corruption in Liberia. Ask an ordinary Liberian about corruption and poor governance. He or she will give you a list of corrupt practices in both the public and the private sectors. He or she will also tell you about how administrations in the past and present have governed Liberia. Unfortunately, ordinary Liberians and even the church are involved in corrupt practices as well.

A definition proposed by the World Bank in 1992 defines governance as the way power is exercised in managing a country's economic and social resources for development.[6] On the other hand, corruption has been defined as an illegal activity conducted through misuse of authority or power by public or private officeholders for private gain and benefits, financial or otherwise.[7] Corruption has persisted throughout the Liberian government, and the World Bank's most recent Worldwide Governance Indicators reflect

---

4. Ozturk, "Role of Education."
5. Zacharias, "Hebrew, Romans and Greeks."
6. Kaufmann and Kraay, "Governance Indicators," 5.
7. Bahoo et al., "Corruption in International Business."

that corruption is still a serious problem in Liberia, unfortunately.[8] Corruption and corrupt perceptions can be considered cultural phenomena because they depend on how society understands the rules and what constitutes a deviation.[9] The unprecedented high levels of corruption in both the public and private sectors and poor governance have destroyed most of Liberia's infrastructures and rendered the national economy unable to invest in education and nation-building adequately.

Corruption has a disproportionate impact on the poor and most vulnerable, increasing costs and reducing access to services, including health, education, and justice. It erodes trust in government and undermines the social construct. Every stolen dollar, euro, peso, yuan, rupee, or ruble robs the poor of an equal opportunity in life and prevents governments from investing in their human capital.[10]

Three Decades of Civil Unrest

Between 1980 and 2003, Liberia experienced a period of different conflicts and national unrest. During this period, the country's health, education, and other basic services were mostly disrupted and severely damaged, leaving the economy fragile or enfeeble. During the civil crisis, buildings were destroyed by armed forces or shell fire, and the contents of homes were either stolen or destroyed.

The devastations caused by fifteen years of civil unrest, which ended three decades ago, did not only hinder Liberia's ability to reduce or eradicate illiteracy from its population, but it also moved the country further ahead on the list of countries with high illiteracy rates and made it more difficult for young Liberians to achieve quality education in their own country. As a result, some Liberians, especially determined Liberians, both young and old, who value education as the most secure means to a successful and independent living have no other options but to seek admissions to colleges and universities in other African countries, the United States of America, Russia, China, and other continents like Europe and Australia.

Even though there have been small efforts made to improve education at some level by previous administrations, much more needs to be accomplished if Liberia is to be positioned on a path of reducing illiteracy amongst its citizens. Unfortunately, the challenge to rebuild all sectors of the country due to the civil crisis is making it increasingly difficult to achieve this goal

---

8. Lee-Jones, "Liberia: Overview."
9. Melgar et al., "Perception of Corruption."
10. "Combating Corruption.".

any time soon. However, the achievement of a lower illiteracy rate in Liberia can be realized or achieved if the national government and ordinary Liberians cultivate a new attitude toward the importance of education and stop blaming their failures to prioritize education on the civil war and those who perpetrated it. The time for shifting blame has long come and gone. All of us must take responsibility for the underdevelopment of the country and its educational system. We must seek ways to forge ahead with transforming how we live and conduct ourselves for the betterment of all Liberians.

Studies show that there are countries in Sub-Saharan Africa, Europe, Asia, and the United States that have gone through civil unrest, economic downturns, and infrastructural destructions but bounced back and are doing economically well. If these countries could successfully reconstruct their infrastructure, socioeconomic and human resource developments, education, health, culture, and tradition, Liberia can also. Our individual and collective willingness and ability to undertake these noble tasks rest in the preparedness and will of all Liberians and not the national government alone.

THE DEPARTURE OF THE OLD MAN AND HIS SON

As they walked throughout the open floor of the dark forest, they kept talking with each other about the interactions they had with the old man and his son. Kerkula and the others wanted to know from Uncle Nat exactly what he and the old man had talked about. They were also interested in knowing from him why the old man had chosen not to speak English throughout the walk until at the end. Uncle Nat tried to educate them on some cultural and traditional norms responsible for the old man's attitude, but the more he talked with them, the more confused they became. Therefore, he was forced to change the subject and began to talk about the journey ahead.

Darkness filled the earth as the four friends traveled through the pitch-black forest. At one point, the girl with them became afraid and questioned Uncle Nat's ability to lead them to where they were going. She was not sure if he knew exactly where he was taking them. Therefore, she decided to ask him. "Do you know where you are taking us, especially this night? I would like to know how many years it has been since you visited your hometown that you would know how easy it is to get there during these dark hours." Apparently, she had an unfortunate experience with Uncle Nat before on similar travels during one of the youth mission trips a couple of years back.

Once upon a time, the girl and some members of the youth group had traveled along with Uncle Nat, the youth president at the time to a youth convention in Boduala ("bo-dua-la"), a remote village across the St. Paul River in lower Bong County. She vividly remembered how they had come to a stop along the way and did not know which road to take because the usual way to the town had been temporarily closed because there was a traditional societal event, which was going on in the village that they had to go through to get to the site of the convention. At this roadblock, Uncle Nat had suggested they come with him on another road, which would have led them to the convention site. According to her, he convinced them that he knew exactly where he was taking them. Unfortunately, they were lost in the forest for two and a half hours before they made it to town.

As usual, Uncle Nat, who was never troubled by critics or concerns others had about him or his ability to undertake tasks, responded in a calm voice as they walked in the dark. He kept assuring them that he knew exactly where they were going and how to get them there. They could not see the reactions on each other's faces because the darkness was too thick. Therefore, they kept on walking and talking quietly to stay alert and listen to others' and animals' sounds and movements along the way.

CHAPTER TWO

What Happens When Tradition Clashes with Civility

Respecting tradition means believing in the sacred nature of the customs handed over through generations and that now organize social life.

—GALLAND AND LEMEL

THEY HAD WALKED FOR approximately one hour after they had separated from the old man and his son before reaching the crossing point at the Yeeli (Yea-la) River where the raft was located. From a few yards, you could see the crossing point ahead. The path which led to it was wider and clear but had a few saplings and tall trees along the riverbanks. The land was flat, and one could see from afar across the other side of the river. No one was found on the side of the river where Kerkula, Uncle Nat, and the other two had arrived.

The evening had come, and it seemed everyone had already come to the riverside and crossed over to the village. The only raft found at the crossing point was the one which the villagers used daily. It was being pulled by the man designated to remove it from the river at the close of the day. Each day when all the villagers had returned home from their respective farms or errands, the raft was pulled from the waters by a designated villager and stored safely on the village side of the river. This was meant to keep it safe and ready for the next day and to prevent thieves from taking it away.

The raft was the only means of transportation on the water by which the villagers conducted trade and commerce, farming, and other errands on the other side of the river. It played a significant role in the movements of people back and forth. Even though other crossing points along the riverbanks were either further down or up the river, those crossing points had their own sets of rafts or canoes to transport their villagers and visitors. If the raft was damaged or underwent major repairs, it meant the villagers were stranded, and their movements across the river were practically halted for the meantime. Those who had to travel did so by either traveling up or down the riverbanks to use the other crossing points.

THE CROSSING POINT

They reached the crossing point in time before the gentleman completely pulled the raft from the river. Uncle Nat was the first who spotted the man pulling the raft because he led them to the riverbanks. "Excuse me, sir," Uncle Nat called out to the man.

But the man replied harshly in Bassa, "What do you want?"

"We need to get to the other side of the river; it is getting late, and we have a long way to go," Uncle Nat responded.

"I am sorry, it is too late now for you to use this raft. Come back tomorrow or go down the river on the other side, and you will find a raft to cross," the man replied, once again in a harsh tone of voice. It seemed he was becoming agitated and vociferous as he began to talk to himself and forcefully pulled the raft from the river.

Throughout the conversation between Uncle Nat and the man, Kerkula and the others stood speechless because they could not understand what both men talked about. They tried to follow hand movements and body language, but the movements and talks were swift at one time and unrecognizable at another. They could only assume Uncle Nat and the man at the crossing were negotiating how to get them across on the other side of the river.

The man's actions did not deter Uncle Nat and the others. They had experienced such behavior before. Moreover, they believed in the African adage that says, "He who has his interest across the river, the seat of his pants is always wet." They knew using the raft to cross the river at that crossing point was the only option they could accept because darkness was upon them. Therefore, all other suggestions made by the man other than taking them across on the raft were unimportant.

They pleaded with the man even more, when they noticed that he was defiantly serious and unwilling to bring the raft back on the other side of the river to help them. Normally, in some villages along riverbanks, no one can cross onto the other side or be transported when the rafts or canoes are removed from the rivers. The safety of the villagers and visitors is a major concern and the reason such a decision is made. However, there are exceptions. In medical emergencies or when an individual of authority like an elder, town chief, or paramount chief must travel, the raft is used no matter the lateness of time.

The more they pleaded with the man, the angrier he became. He screamed loud and louder at the top of his lungs in his native dialect each time they called on him to come back across the river and transport them.

Astonishingly, the girl with them noticed that the rope connected to the raft was still tied to a small tree on the side of the river where they were standing. The robe was submerged, which made it a little difficult to see from a distance. It showed why the man on the other side of the river found it increasingly difficult to pull the raft out from the river at once. The raft was tied on both sides of the river to allow villagers and visitors from either side to access it during the crossing hours.

Suddenly, the girl began to yell, "Uncle Nat! Uncle Nat! Look, the raft is still tied over here."

"Where?" Uncle Nat asked.

"Right there!" She exclaimed. By this time, Uncle Nat's eyes lighted, and he became emotional as though a miracle had just happened. He ran to the tree where the rope which was tied to the raft was connected. He pulled the rope and realized that it was indeed connected to the raft. Immediately, he began to pull the raft to himself and soon encounter resistance from the man pulling on the other side. He pleaded with the man once more to allow them to use the raft to cross the river, but he refused. At this point, Uncle Nat was not sure if the man was going to allow them to cross to the other side of the river. Again, it was getting late, and returning to the village where they had already passed three hours ago was not a good idea. They were not willing to go back; they had to cross the river.

Uncle Nat began to pull harder and harder to bring the raft to him, but the man was just too strong to allow him to pull the raft away. The others quickly joined him, and they pulled the raft on their side of the river. They got on and pulled to the other side as quickly as they could. By this time, the man had left the riverbanks and ran to town. No one knew what he was doing and why he had abandoned the raft at the crossing point. Kerkula and the others arrived in town shortly after leaving the riverbanks.

The town was a little quiet, with few people moving around and trying to settle in for the night. Uncle Nat suggested that they find some food to eat and a place to spend the night before continuing their journey the next day. They saw an elderly lady making food under a palava hut nearby and went to see her.

"Do you have food to sell?" Uncle Nat asked the woman in Bassa.

He assumed she spoke the dialect, but she quickly responded in Kpelle, another dialect spoken by other villagers. "No, I do not have food for sale, but I can give you and your friends some of my food to eat," the woman replied. "It seems you and your friends have been traveling a long distance and are hungry."

Uncle Nat became bemused because he did not understand what the woman had said. Immediately, the girl with them interpreted what the woman had said. "Great! We would love some food to eat," Uncle Nat added. They took a seat under the palava hut and began to enjoy the warmth of the firewood as the woman prepared the food.

THE FIRST ENCOUNTER

All seemed to be going well, and Uncle Nat started to negotiate with the lady about accommodations for him and his friends to spend the night. Suddenly, the so-called raft man, as Uncle Nat and the others referred to him, showed up closer to the palava hut and began pointing his fingers at them. He spoke again in Bassa, saying, "These are the people who forced the raft from my hands and came across the river. They must be enemy soldiers." Some villagers, especially men, immediately began to move toward the palava hut where they were sitting. They confronted Uncle Nat and asked him about the situation. As he tried to explain what happened, the so-called raft man became upset and started raising his voice, just as he had at the riverside. He paced back and forth, rubbing his hands together vehemently as an expression of his anger. At one point, he kicked a bucket of warm bath water, which the older woman had prepared for the girl who was traveling with them to take her evening bath before bed. The bucket was positioned next to one of the pillars of the palava hut where they were seated.

The sound of his voice drew more and more people to the palava hut. By this time, Kerkula and the others were becoming concerned and feared the worse was about to happen. Uncle Nat seemed not to be frightened or moved by either the crowd's movements or the actions of the so-called raft man. Kerkula and the others realized they were in a strange town and did not know anyone to talk with concerning the situation. Additionally, they did not know the community or terrain where they were. The lady whose palava hut they were seated at was the only one they had interacted with apart from the so-called raft man.

THE VISIT OF A PROMINENT TRADITIONAL PERSONALITY

While the talks were ongoing between Uncle Nat and the men who had come to confront him, suddenly what sounded like a trumpet echoed throughout the town. The voice doubled and was swift as the movement of people became sporadic. It emanated from the northern side of the village and spread far and wide. It was the voice of a man who was known by the villagers as the "town crier." Like the shofars (horns used in ancient Israel at important Jewish public and religious occasions), the town crier's voice was unique and authoritative. The sound of his voice was meant to assemble all villagers to an important meeting or alert them about the visitation of a societal elite, a personality with high authority and influence.

"Kehyoo ('keh-yoo')! Kehyoo!" His voice sounded for the second time. These words were spoken in Bassa and used to introduce a traditional societal figure who was usually referred to by the locals as "Gbetu" ("gbe-tu"), or "Country Devil."

He was highly respected, and his presence demanded all who came in his presence or heard about his arrival to town had to be humbled. His entry into the village was so majestically electrifying that it forced Uncle Nat and the others, including villagers who were considered nonmembers of his entourage or societal group, to seek refuge in huts built with sticks and mud and kitchens with bamboo branches rooftops.

No one could come into his presence or peep at him through the crack of doors, windows, or whatever if he or she were not a member of his entourage or the societal group. It was forbidden for nonmembers to come out or be anywhere in the vicinity when he visited a town. Nonmembers who traveled from nearby towns or who were returning home from their farms enroute to the village where he was had to either go a different road or stay away from the village until his visit was over and he had left the town.

You may wonder why he had a masculine and not a feminine gender. The reason is simple. Upon his arrival in the village and during his stay, no female was out and about or allowed to come out; only men were allowed.

This was a clear manifestation that only men could come in his presence because he was a man.

He visited the village for approximately fifteen to twenty minutes and departed suddenly to the southwest side of the town, the same route he had used to enter. His presence in the village was significantly felt to the extent that you could drop a penny and hear it make a sound. The clouds darkened and the trees stood still as he moved from one side of the village to the next. Even the animals became quiet as he and his entourage engaged each other. For this book and to honor the village cultural heritage, traditions, and people, discussions of this powerful personality will be limited.

Upon his departure, villagers and visitors, including Uncle Nat and the others, were permitted to come outside. Uncle Nat went up to a gentleman who sat next to the palava hut where they had stood prior to the Country Devil's arrival in town and inquired about the reason for his visit. The man informed Uncle Nat and the others that the Gbetu came to town to deal with the raft-crossing situation between the "raft man" and a stranger but decided to leave town after the elders told him they would handle the issue themselves. It was apparent that the man who spoke with Uncle Nat about the purpose of the Devil's visit did not know who he was, or else he might not have told him what had happened.

THE SECOND ENCOUNTER

Uncle Nat and Kerlula were frightened that a situation so trivial could demand the presence of such a prominent traditional personality and member of the village. This was the first time in many years for Kerkula to have seen his friend, Uncle Nat, become so frightened. As they tried to settle back under the palava hut for the second time, the so-called raft man returned once again and started pointing his fingers and making lots of accusations against them.

He demanded that Uncle Nat be brought in the town square and have the Country Devil come out again and speak with him concerning what had happened at the crossing point. Neither Uncle Nat, Kerkula, nor either of the other two was willing to come into the presence of this highly respected personality. Neither Uncle Nat nor Kerkula was a member of any society or traditional group. However, the girl and the other boy were both members of the Poro and Sande societies. The Poro and Sande societies are traditionally male and female societies that teach and train young boys and girls to become better fathers and mothers in society.

What Happens When Tradition Clashes with Civility

One would think when there was a civil dispute, there would be a civil resolution. Unfortunately, this is not how it works most of the time in a typical traditional setting, especially in a traditionally influenced African or Liberian village where the power of culture and tradition often transcends modern civilization or the advocacy for civility. For decades, it has been an environment in which the advocacy for civilization or civility is often regarded as corruptible or referred to as a Western culture or way of life. Interestingly, some conflicts that are resolved in traditional villages in Liberia are often settled by the elders, paramount chiefs, and/or town chiefs, or sometimes by the Country Devil.

Kerkula quickly realized that the situation was getting out of hand and they needed to leave the village as soon as possible. Even though it was not yet late, the village was no longer a peaceful place to be. Their safety was at stake, and they needed to act quickly before darkness consumed the earth like it did the night before. The lady whose kitchen they were seated under agreed with Kerkula that they needed to either leave the village as soon as possible or find a place to spend the night before the devil returned. She invited them to stay in her house for the night and leave early the next day when the earth awakened from its slumber and the morning dew began to fall on grass and tree branches. "We cannot stay here tonight. We have to continue our journey throughout the night and hopefully make it home by day," Kerkula responded. "We have been walking for the past few hours and have walked for days before; we can't stop walking now. We have to keep on walking until we reach our final destination."

As usual, Uncle Nat took the lead. He led his friends down a narrow path behind the lady's house, a path which she had advised them to take. The path went through a backyard garden into a cassava patch and down through a young bush. They walked as fast as possible to avoid anyone from noticing that they had left town and what direction they were headed. It was a risky decision to leave the village during the evening hours, but they had no choice.

The roads ahead were still farther away and unfamiliar. Therefore, they needed to stay focused and walk through the night to get to the next village before midnight. They could not stop walking. Equally, they were cautious about "freedom fighters'" movements from one village to the next and surrounding areas. They kept quiet as they walked through the dark and narrow paths in the forest. They were mindful of making minimum noise with their feet or with the bags on their backs. They kept their ears open for movements of people, animals, and sounds ahead of and behind them.

Occasionally, they came close to ambushes along the roads, especially car roads which led to other villages or towns. It was difficult at times to identify if you were about to fall in an ambush because they were not visible or could easily be suspected. However, some individuals could easily predict an ambush location, either because they were part of the movement and knew where their fellow fighters were positioned or because they were being informed by someone else who was a fighter and had information about their activities. Those who were freedom fighters could easily detect the positions of ambushes because they had been trained to identify the locations and knew the secret codes or passwords, which were shared amongst them. Those who knew not this information were trapped and often left in life-or-death situations. Knowing about these things helped save innocent lives. Unfortunately, others had lost their lives because they did not know about warfare or took situations for granted.

THE NEXT VILLAGE

They walked throughout the early part of the night about three hours before reaching the next village. There were not many movements of people or activities going on in this village upon arrival. Most of the villagers were already asleep. A handful of men walked around while the others were seated under the kitchen, warming themselves around blazing firewood. Some were drinking bamboo/palm wine and goat soup, while others were smoking tobacco in wooden pipes made locally. Like the previous village with the "raft man," there were no females out in any corner of this town accept the girl with Kerkula and Uncle Nat.

Traditionally, when men gather at night under palava huts or a rice kitchen and discuss "men's business," the females are usually at home attending to the children or asleep. Like the men, the females also have time to discuss what concerns them and their families. They, too, are left alone to discuss amongst themselves without any man's involvement when such a time becomes necessary. This is typical of a normal, culturally unified Liberian village in which everyone is his or her brother's keeper.

Unfortunately, during the civil unrest, some villagers were forced to adapt self-centered and egotistic behaviors against a unified village approach for several reasons, including the scarcity of basic human necessities (like food, shelter, and clothing), fears of intimidation and harassment, conscription of their children, abuse (sexual, physical, verbal, financial, or material), false accusation, and exploitation. Villagers had to do things the other way to protect the little they had left for them and their families.

As Kerkula and the others approached the kitchen where the men were seated, one of them who was the first to see Uncle Nat upon arrival in the village stood up and walked directly toward him. He had assumed these were fighters entering their town. Therefore, he wanted to confront them early before things got out of hand. During the civil war, some villages and towns were always on the alert for visitors who traveled periodically in and out of their village or town. These towns and villages established what became known as "Citizens or Community Defense Force" (CDF), which was comprised of local boys and men who voluntarily or involuntarily joined organized groups to defend their towns and villages against those who came to commit atrocities against them and their families.

The gentleman walked up to Kerkula and said, "Were you the man who pulled the raft back across the river when it was time to close the crossing point?"

"No, sir!" Kerkula responded. "I think you are mistaking me for someone else."

Before he could utter another word, Uncle Nat interrupted him and said, "No one pulled the raft from the river, sir. My friends and I saw a man at the crossing point and asked him to help us get on the other side of the river, but he insisted that he was not going to help us. Fortunately for us, the rope which was connected to the raft was still connected on our side of the river. Therefore, we decided to get on and cross because it was getting late and we had nowhere to go. Going back to where we came from as suggested by the man was not an option for us. Sir, we had been walking all day and just wanted to get some rest in the town by the river before getting back on the roads." Uncle Nat continued, "Honestly, we did not go to that village to start any troubles; we just wanted to get across the river and head home."

"That is not what we were told. I think you are lying to us," one of the men in the kitchen uttered. "He is not lying, sir," Kerkula said. "That is exactly what happened."

"It doesn't matter what happened, but just be aware, it cannot happen in this village, or else you and your friends will not live to tell the story," the gentleman cautioned.

It was clear that what had happened in the village by the riverbanks had already been revealed by someone in the village where Uncle Nat and the others had come from. It frightened them to know that someone from the other village by the river was already ahead of them and had spread the wrong information. Therefore, they decided not to spend a longer time in the town but to continue their walk immediately. They asked the man who had come up to them for directions, and he was kind to assist them. They bided them goodbye and started their walk once again.

They slipped behind an old rice kitchen into the dark while the man was still talking to himself as though they were still standing right in front of him. The late-night creatures whispered throughout the dark forests as the soothing breeze blew against their foreheads. The sounds of owls, creeping insects, and singing night birds in the surrounding trees were heard closer and in the distance. Fear was irresistible as the moonlight faded away and darkness consumed the forest. They had no lights to walk with but depended on night flies, which spread their wings during flights and partially illuminated the areas. They followed each other closely along the pathways to maintain connection and a steady pace. When anyone stopped, everyone stopped, and when anyone talked, everyone listened. It was no time for them to argue or fight with each other. The forest had become too unfamiliar and scary; they needed each other's support and confidence to make it through. At one point during the walk, Uncle Nat admitted that the fear of the dark forest was becoming unbearable, and he had hoped they would come into a town quickly, but it took a while before they did. That is how they kept walking throughout the night until they finally reached their destination.

CHAPTER THREE

New Life in a Strange Town

Every adversity, every failure, every headache carries with it the seed of an equal or greater benefit.

—Napoleon Hill

The rising sun in the northern part of the town greeted them early the next morning as they finally entered the village that Uncle Nat had always called home. The town seemed quiet and desolate. There were not many people in the village, but a few were either getting ready to go to their farms or were late going to work in the gold mines. Some villagers took the day off and hung around in town, while others conducted smaller in-house businesses, like selling dried gin (aka cane juice), cigarettes, snuff, or cooked food (aka cooked bowls).

A few chickens and goats were running the streets and kids were playing; under one of the palava huts, which was diagonal to where the kids were, there was an older man wearing a traditional Liberian gown sitting in front of his house on a small bamboo bench. The house was painted white and had a large rock before it. Long after their stay in the village, they learned that the rock in front of the house was there for a reason. No one could sit on or remove it. It was believed that the rock held the secrets to confessions. Those who had committed mysterious acts like witchcraft or secret murder would come to the rock and confess before he or she died. The villagers believed the rock was meant to give those involved in these practices the opportunity to confront their sin and seek forgiveness from the town's victims and elders before they died. That way, they would not die in sin or without forgiveness.

Uncle Nat took his friends to his brother's house since there was nowhere else for them to go or anyone to talk with. *Knock, knock!* He pounded on the front door, but no one responded. *Knock, knock!* he banged the door for the second time, and no one responded again.

"He is not there; he and his wife went to the farm beyond the hills this morning," sounded a clear voice in Bassa from across the walkway that separated his brother's house from another house on the other side of the street. It was an older man standing in the window and looking onto the streets. The older man later became known as "Na Ne Po" ("na-ne-po"). He was one of the elders and church leaders who was highly respected by his fellow villagers and visitors alike. He was also a dignified authority and leading voice in the traditional society. He usually sat behind his open window and stared at his fellow villagers who walked by daily. This became a daily routine for him because he had retired from farming due to his age and had a major traditional role as previously mentioned in the village.

He spoke with distinct influence and had a good sense of humor. He knew how to captivate his audience, young and old, by telling intriguing jokes and parables. One of the notable parables he always told was "a red deer with one eye cannot see flashlight beams." He was a good hunter and did more hunting when he was much younger. He had learned the behaviors and movements of animals in the forest. He always believed that deer, in general, had a unique challenge with flashlight beams. Apparently, flashlight beams seemed to blind the eyes of a deer at night, making it much easier for a hunter to kill it. Therefore, he believed red deer with only one eye were usually at a greater disadvantage of seeing clearly when a flashlight was pointed in their eyes by a hunter, especially at night.

"Gboweh ('gbo-weh'), is that you?" the older man said in Bassa.

"Yes, uncle, it is I!" Uncle Nat responded in Bassa also.

"Where are you coming from, and why are you home?" The older man questioned.

"My friends and I just arrived in town from Bong Mines. We have been walking for the past three days because of a war in our area."

"Thank God you made it home safely. Your father was here this morning, but he and his wife left for the farm," the older man lamented. "I am not sure if he is coming home anytime soon. It would be better for you and your friends to go to him on the farm. I am sure he would be glad to see you again after all these years." He repositioned his bamboo chair at the window, pulled out a piece of kola nut from the front pocket of his African gown and took a bite as he smiled at Uncle Nat. "Go ahead and find your father,

Gboweh. We will talk later when you get back to town tonight. Come back and find me, so I can tell you all that had happened to me over the years, and you can tell me yours."

Rev. G.G. Garpue was often referred to as Uncle Nat's father because he was the oldest and the only surviving sibling to him. Traditionally, when the father of a family dies, the oldest son automatically assumes or is expected to lead the rest of the surviving family as their father or head of the family. This is a typical ancestral arrangement or family norm in most Liberian families, which has been in existence for decades.

SAYE WHEH TOWN

Once upon a time, when Uncle Nat was a little boy and growing up in the village, the elders, including the older man, usually called him "Gboweh," which is the name of the mourning dove in Bassa. As a young boy, Uncle Nat was hardworking but hardheaded. His oldest brother would often talk about his growing up during conversations with others and how much he loved and cared about his younger brother when he lived in the village. He also spoke about how often he had to rescue him from domestic disputes and other problems. Nevertheless, he always praised him for being God-fearing, generous to others, and hardworking.

Uncle Nat and his friends decided not to go see his brother on the farm, as suggested by the older man, because they were tired. Walking throughout the night without food and water made them exhausted. Therefore, they settled on the front porch of his brother's house for a while and later went to a neighbor's kitchen where they had been invited to eat some food and take baths while they waited for his brother and his family to return from the farm. After lunch and spending time at the next-door neighbor's kitchen, Uncle Nat decided to take his friends for a walk around the town, since there was still more time for his brother and his family to return home.

Saye Wheh Town is a small, multi-tribal, multi-cultural village located in Kokoyah District, upper Bong County. The name Saye Wheh is from the Mano tribe, one of three tribal groups which constitute the town's original inhabitants. "Saye" is the name given to the first male child in a Mano family, who, by tradition, is his father's successor upon his demise. Saye Wheh Town was established by Mr. Saye Wheh Zackpah, a young man who migrated from Nimba County in northern Liberia to Kokoyah, Bong County. According to one of his surviving daughters, her father was a gifted and brave warrior who had many children. He was highly respected by many of his compatriots and those who opposed him and detested his way of life.

He was a courageous and fearless warrior who went after his enemies and anyone who sought to commit atrocities against his people. It is believed that he came to what is now known as Saye Wheh Town in the late 1800s in search of better living opportunities and with a drive to establish a town of his own. After successfully establishing his town, he helped other northeastern Liberians who came his way to establish towns of their own. One of several individuals he helped was Mr. David Dean, who later established Dean's Town, another gold mining community.

Saye Wheh Town is few kilometers away from the banks of the St. John River, which runs directly through Bong and Grand Bassa counties and empties into the Atlantic Ocean. The map below shows the source of the St. John River from the northern border between the Republic of Guinea and Liberia. The St. Paul River is one of six major rivers in Liberia and serves as a good source of food (e.g., fishing and water supply) and agriculture (farming and irrigation).

Saye Wheh Town is situated on a semi-hilly land and runs down to creeks, grassy fields, young bushes, and some bamboo plants. The town is accessible from several vantage points and roads leading from different nearby towns, villages, and hillsides. The town is bounded on the west by Bahn's Town, on the east by Gbecon ("gbe-con"), on the north by creeks and hills, and on the south by Dean's Town and gold creeks. Most of the village homes were built with sticks and mud and a few with dirt bricks. The houses built were primarily used as dwelling places with just a few commercial shops where goods were sold. Some homes were also used as points of contact for transacting business, especially with other merchants from other towns and villages who came to sell their products.

New Life in a Strange Town 25

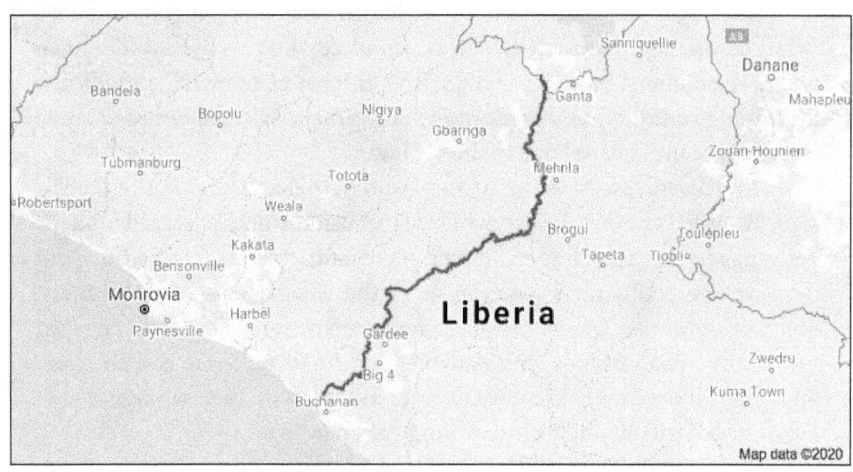

Source: en.wikipedia.org. The St. Paul River in Liberia

The map above illustrates the St. John River headwaters beginning in upper Bong County in the north of Liberia, bordering the Republic of Guinea, and ending south of the Atlantic Ocean.

A transitional mud and stick house in Liberia

The house above is like some of the transitional houses built with sticks, mud, and zinc in Saye Wheh Town. Unlike the old-fashioned palm or bamboo branch rooftops, these were some of the finest houses, built with zinc roofs in the past or during those days. Either one is preferable by reputable or financially stable residents of the village.

According to reliable sources, including sons and daughters of Saye Wheh Town, approximately five to six hundred villagers lived in the town before the outburst of the civil crisis. The number of residents sporadically increased to one thousand or more, including those who had returned home forcefully or unprepared due to the civil war.

There were also freedom fighters who patrolled in and out of the village, displaced families who sought refuge, businessmen (e.g., gold brokers, gold diggers, tobacco traders, textile merchants, traders, etc.) who spent days, weeks, and sometimes months in the village transacting business. Some businessmen and visitors became permanent residents and engaged in romantic relationships with daughters of the town. Some had children, and others moved away to other towns or villages with their wives and husbands or boyfriends and girlfriends to begin new lives.

Even though Saye Wheh Town is rich in minerals, culture, and traditional heritage, it was unfortunately inaccessible by roads for moving machineries like airplanes, large trucks, or motor vehicles. The limited road network leading to and from the town was not in good condition for vehicles to travel. One had to travel long distances either by foot or in the cars that took the risk to travel to the town. There was a shortage of vehicles (privately owned) that traveled to the village. Most vehicles that went back and forth during the war were owned and operated by fighters. It was almost unusual to see a privately owned vehicle during the war unless the owner was directly connected or associated with a senior officer of the movement.

However, this does not mean that citizens of Saye Wheh Town could not afford to purchase vehicles. They could purchase more vehicles if they wanted to because they had the money or minerals to purchase whatever they wanted. Unfortunately, owning and operating private vehicles during the civil crisis was not a prudent thing to do. Private vehicle owners were at risk of their vehicles being confiscated, harassments, intimidation, or even brutality if they decided to operate a vehicle amid the civil crisis. Moreover, it was even risky for a private owner to resist confiscation by an individual carrying a gun who demanded his or her vehicle. Therefore, it was prudent not to even venture to put a private vehicle on the roads. Still, private vehicles that were not on the roads but kept on private properties were confiscated or looted by gunmen.

Typical traditional huts built in Liberia with bamboo or palm branch rooftops

The picture above shows two distinct buildings with different purposes. Both buildings are traditionally built with sticks, mud, and bamboo branches. They are typically found in most Liberian villages. The building on the left is mostly used as a dwelling place while the building on the right is used as a kitchen and storage for food items, farm products and equipment, and other essentials that the villagers often use daily.

Traditional home in Liberia built with mud, sticks, and bamboo mat.

This house is symbolic of the conversion from traditional homes built with sticks, mud, and palm or bamboo branch rooftops to homes built with zinc roofs and wooden windows. House like this were common in Saye Wheh Town during the civil war.

This is one of two gravel roads which lead directly into Saye Wheh Town—
Kokoyah District, Bong County, Liberia.

CHAPTER FOUR

Reshaping the Minds of the Youth amid a Civil War

Five percent of the people think; ten percent of the people think they think; and the other eighty-five percent would rather die than think.

—Thomas Edison

Some people assent to the notion that wars are started by wise men but fought by fools. Herbert Hoover, thirty-first president of the United States, believed, "Older men declare wars, but it is the youth who must fight and die."[1] Studies have shown that women, children, and the elderly are the most vulnerable population of any warfare fought internally or externally. These individuals are most likely to suffer the continual impacts of warfare, even when the physical battle is long over.

The impacts of warfare, especially on children or any nation's youth, cannot be overemphasized or underestimated. From the Philippines to Syria, Afghanistan to Iraq, Yemen to Libya, Rwanda to Sudan, the Democratic Republic of the Congo to Somalia, and Liberia to Sierra Leone, children have been exploited and victimized by those who seek unconstitutional power and authority through the barrels of the gun or by the use of other forceful and violent ventures. This is a moral issue that has been overlooked or swept under the rug for decades by countries globally.

1. Gould and Cheng, "Wise Quotes on Life."

Global governments' failures to acknowledge and find individual and/or collective remedies to these issues have impacted and continue to impact their national interests directly or indirectly.

War leaves indelible imprints on any human being's physical, psychological, mental, intellectual, and spiritual faculties, but most especially on those of the youth. This is true because youths are expected or assumed to live longer lives than their adult parents. As a result, they carry the indelible imprints of warfare on their minds, in their activities, and engagements throughout their young age and into adulthood. For example, a study conducted by Brandon Kohrt in Nepal found that children associated with fighting forces (e.g., rebel groups, gangs, mercenaries, or guerilla fighters) exhibited moderately higher psychosocial problems (aggression, depression, anxiety, and post-traumatic stress) as compared to never-associated children.[2] Another study conducted by C. P. Bayer and colleagues found that more than one-third, about 34.9 percent, of child soldiers met diagnostic criteria for post-traumatic stress disorder (PTSD).[3]

Children are victims who must live through the memories of the abuse and atrocities they have endured and/or perpetuated against those who have fallen victims to their actions. Children may be subjected to horrific abuses in war zones, including sexual violence and abduction. They may be trained to use deadly weapons or exploited as cooks, messengers, and sex slaves. Many young boys and girls were brutalized into submission, drugged, and then forced to fight on the front lines of combat; others who did not fight served as porters, cooks, guards, messengers, servants, human shields, or bush "wives."[4]

A child's innocence should never be used as a weapon to abuse, destroy, or subject him or her to an unproductive and abnormal way of life. Every child deserves a chance in life. Therefore, it is imperative for society to provide opportunities that will ensure that each child is given a chance and not deprived. Unfortunately, children's abuse due to the lack of knowledge and protection from society has been recorded with little or nothing being done to the perpetrators. Children below the age of eighteen years constitute more than 50 percent of most countries affected by war and are among the most vulnerable, unable to protect themselves from its impact.[5]

In 2014, the special representative of the secretary-general for Children and Armed Conflict and the United Nations Children Fund (UNICEF)

---

2. Kohrt, "Recommendations to Promote."
3. Bayer et al., "Association of Trauma," 558.
4. Betancourt et al., "Sierra Leone's Former Child Soldiers," 2.
5. "Children, Not Soldiers."

initiated a campaign under the banner, "Children, Not Soldiers."[6] The campaign was intended to solicit a global consensus to abolish children or child soldiers in war or civil conflicts internally or externally. Even though the campaign ended in December 2016, it succeeded in convincing about eight countries that have been noted by UNICEF for recruiting children and using them in their internal conflicts. The countries included the Democratic Republic of the Congo, Somalia, Southern Sudan, Chad, Afghanistan, Yemen, and Myanmar.

The 2007 Paris Principles established the definition of a child associated with an armed force or armed group as "any person below 18 years of age who is or who has been recruited or used by an armed force or armed group in any capacity, including but not limited to children, boys and girls, used as fighters, cooks, porters, messengers, spies or for sexual purposes. It does not only refer to a child who is taking or has taken a direct part in hostilities."[7]

No doubt anyone would be interested in knowing how the mindset of a youth carrying guns amid a civil war can be reshaped or changed from engaging in hostilities that they have become accustomed to becoming productive citizens and nation builders. This was the question that Kerkula and Uncle Nat had to contemplate for days and even weeks to find suitable answers. Both men were convinced that they had to initiate a plan to change the youth's mindset in Saye Wheh Town from indulging in warfare and hostilities to becoming more productive and civil villagers. They knew a successful change of the youth meant a long-lasting violence-free community because a negative mindset controls who we are. Unfortunately, "there is only so much room in a brain, so much wall space as it were, and if you furnish it with your slogans, the opposition has no place to put up any pictures later on, because the apartment of the brain is already crowded with furniture."[8]

As humans, we control our minds, but our mindset controls us. This is evident by the way we think and the things we say and do. Uncle Nat and his friend knew from the beginning of their planning that it would not have been an easy task to reshape the youth's minds because they were deeply involved with warfare and making money from gold mining. They had become indoctrinated and led into believing a new way of life contrary to their ancestral beliefs or conventional wisdom. They had been made to believe that their survival and strength depended on themselves, those in authority

---

6. "Children, Not Soldiers."
7. Betancourt et al., "Sierra Leone's Former Child Soldiers," 7.
8. Field, "Biographical Sketches."

of their respective movements, and their abilities to pull the trigger at will on the weapons they carried.

Jeremiah 17:5-6 reminds us that "cursed is the man who trusts in a man and makes flesh his strength, whose heart turns away from the Lord. He is like a shrub in the desert and shall not see when good comes. He shall dwell in the parched places of the wilderness, in an uninhabited salt land" (ESV). Proverbs 28:26 says, "Whosoever trusts in his mind is a fool, but he who walks in wisdom will be delivered" (NIV). Proverbs 29:25 says, "The fear of man lays a snare, but whosoever trusts in the Lord is safe" (ESV).

Arguably, young people who fought in the civil war in Liberia were successful on the front lines by their abilities to easily capture villages, towns, and cities with little or no resistance whatsoever. They possessed and exhibited enormous power and authority warranted to take away innocent individuals' lives with no or fewer reprimands whatsoever from their superiors. They could order a person to move or be removed, sit or be forced to sit, commit improper acts or lose their lives. However, they did not realize that they were losing their mental faculties, the ability to discern right from wrong and good from evil. If not most of them, some were constantly under the influence of drugs, alcohol, and/or possessed by demonic powers.

They were also influenced by a catchword, "San-ga-lay-go-wa," which means, "You come against us and fail; we come against you and win." A catchword gives the unthinking mob the material for an idea and furnishes them with the pleasant illusion that they are thinking themselves. This slogan was developed or adapted from the onset of the rebel invasion and used throughout the war. "San-ga-lay-go-wa" was widely used by the fighters, both old and young, males and females. There was always some sort of action or excitement exhibited by a fighter or group of fighters at the mention of the word. "San-ga-lay-go-wa" will go down in the history books of Liberia as one of the deadliest influential phrases ever used to galvanize and incite people into taking violent actions against innocent people and the state. It surpassed the impacts of the phrase, "In the cause of the people, the struggle continues," which was often used by the Progress Alliance of Liberia (PAL) and the Movement for Justice in Africa (MOJA) during the 1980s.

During the initial reshaping process of the youth in Saye Wheh Town who were actively engaged in the use of weapons amid the civil war, Kerkula and Uncle Nat had to first disarm or change their mentality from negativity, in which they considered life as non-essential, to positivity, in which they recognized life as a right given by the creator that should never be taken away by another human being. In his letter to the Romans, the apostle Paul, in chapter 12:2, said, "Do not conform to the pattern of this world but be transformed by the renewing of your mind. Then you will be able to test and approve what God's will is, his good, pleasing, and perfect will." Also, in Romans 8:7, Paul writes, "For the mind that is set on the flesh is hostile to God, for it does not submit to God's law; indeed, it cannot." The youth who carried and operated guns amid the civil war lacked or ignored the power of God to save them. Therefore, they depended on other gods and supernatural powers for protection and guidance. They also sought guidance and parenthood from the adults who conjured them into becoming child soldiers. Their failure to honor and trust God led them to disregard his creation—mankind. As a result, death became a public cry, torture, and intimidation, a national display.

During the civil crisis, renewing the youth's mindset to think positively was not an option given by those who controlled, used, and abused them. They were held hostage mentally by the adults whom they believed and trusted for guidance. They were misled into believing that their newly found freedom, wrongful exercise of authority, and power that had no or less reprimand from their superiors was a better way of life than living the normal traditional or cultural ways their parents had taught them. It, therefore, became urgent that someone help them reshape their mindset and restore them to their sanity.

How could the youth emulate their adult parents' good characters when there were none to emulate? All they saw was violence and hatred. How could they see the best in themselves when they did not see the best in those whom they looked up to, trusted, and regarded as parents or adults? How could they bring out the best in themselves when the best they were taught was against themselves? How could they have enjoyed their youth when it was stolen from them? How could they have known what it meant to be a youth when all they knew was how to play adults' roles? Paul reminds us in 2 Corinthians 10:5 that "we demolish arguments and every pretension that sets itself up against the knowledge of God, and we take captive every thought to make it obedient to Christ" (NIV).

Kerkula and Uncle Nat knew upon arrival in the town that something had to be done quickly with the village youth to prevent the town from disintegrating into a community of lawless individuals looking out for themselves instead of the entire village. They feared the worst would have happened if a proactive plan and engagement with the youth were not initiated; they would have experienced the same hostilities they had endured in Bong Mines and throughout their walk to the village. They considered first working with the youth in the town as the best strategy for their plan. They considered it a top priority and the best way to begin their engagements with the youth and villagers. Both men believed their strategy would have provided better options to young people rather than engaging in warfare and hostilities. The plan would have eventually led the youth to convince their parents and elders into believing that their new way of life was a better option for them rather than engaging in fighting against their brothers and sisters who had done them no wrong. This would have encouraged parents to allow their children to work entirely with Uncle Nat and Kerkula without reservations or a second thought of being a freedom fighter. The strategy worked for the most part.

Uncle Nat and Kerkula had a common idea about their planning process because they believed and trusted God for their plan to succeed. They knew the plan would not have succeeded unless they first committed it to God. Therefore, they withdrew from all farm and sporting activities for two weeks, stayed in the village from morning till night, fasted, and prayed. They engaged in light activities like church services and Bible studies, casual conversations, evening walks, and short visits to the farm beyond the hills to gather food. This was done to avoid other villagers suspecting or questioning their motives.

They tried not to be the "Pharisees" of the village by making everyone know they were fasting or engaged in some sort of spiritual activity. They were mindful not to expose their plans to other residents of the town in advance. Therefore, they kept it a secret. They trusted the senior pastor of the church, Uncle Nat's oldest brother, with their plan. Hence, they told him the details, and he endorsed it. Rev. G.G. was thankful that he was finally receiving the assistance he had looked forward to having for decades to help reshape the youth's mindset and spread the gospel throughout the village. He was more optimistic about the future role of the church in the village and surrounding towns because of the new approach and direction the church had embarked upon.

THE TRINITY PLAN

Confronted with the challenges of reshaping the youth's mindset, both men wondered about the successful implementation strategy of their plan. Thoughts of how to commence without making unnecessary mistakes traveled back and forth through their minds. Even though Uncle Nat was a native of the town, he had not lived there for almost three decades. He spent most of his young adult life in Bong Mines with his family but periodically visited his brother and family to help them with the management and operations of the farm, domestic affairs, and partially with the church's activities.

Once upon a time, Uncle Nat worked directly with his brother when he was much younger as a member of the United Methodist Church. This was several decades ago before he decided to become a member of the Lutheran Church in Liberia. He later decided to move to Bong Mines with his family and joined the Holy Cross Lutheran Church.

Unlike Uncle Nat, Kerkula had never visited Saye Wheh Town or heard about it before going there. He had heard about Kokoyah District, but it was his first time visiting a village in the district and spending a long time there.

One evening, just as everyone returned home from their farms and the gold mines, Uncle Nat, Kerkula, and the other two individuals were also headed back to town. They had gone to his brother's farm to gather food for the week. Both men seized the opportunity to begin talks on their plans. First, they considered some of the threats and challenges which could easily disrupt the plans. For example, they thought about the village being surrounded by gold mines and that anyone willing and able to do gold mining could earn a living and did not necessarily have to engage in farming or other sustainable ventures to feed his or her family.

They also considered other challenges, including:

- the fact that villagers, especially the young people, spent more time on gold mines or farms and less time in the village;
- the large import of foreign products brought in the town for sale by local and other merchants who conducted business transactions in other African countries (e.g., Guinea, Ivory Coast, and Sierra Leone);
- the lack of interest by a good percentage of villagers in church activities, and their weekend engagements in social festivals;
- the ease of making money and becoming independent;
- the fact that some youth and adults carried guns and had the exclusive power to exercise their authority at will unquestionably;
- the sporadic entry and exit of vehicles loaded with freedom fighters from other villages and towns;
- the constant fear and rumors of another outbreak of hostilities to be led by another warring faction.

Even though both men were overwhelmed by the magnitude of challenges and threats they identified during the plans' development, they were determined to succeed and bring about the change the church and town needed. They were grateful for the immense opportunities available to them in the village despite everything else—for example, the presence of a local United Methodist Church in the village, the availability of local churches in surrounding villages and towns that they could fellowship with, the willingness of some youth to participate, the possibilities of the two men working in the gold mines and earning income to support the plan, and the unwavering support and approval of the plan by the head pastor.

Apart from the potential problems both men were concern about, the biggest challenge for them remained figuring out how to reshape the minds of young individuals who knew nothing else but hostilities, seeking fortune, and harassing innocent people as a way of survival. Young people saw themselves not as the problem or victims of military movements and organizations who abused their innocence and deprived them of their youth. Instead, they saw themselves as the solution to the problems initiated by their parents, which caused the civil war.

Sun Tzu was right when he said, "If you know the enemy and know yourself, you need not fear the result of a hundred battles. If you know yourself but not the enemy, you will also suffer a defeat for every victory gained. If you know neither the enemy nor yourself, you will succumb in every battle."[9] This was exactly what young people suffered and were going through in this village and around the country. The youth were enemies of themselves and did not know it. They looked at others as enemies and destroyed what would have been the solutions to their problems and the predicaments of all Liberians.

Theodore Roosevelt, twenty-sixth president of the United States, put it right when he said, "War is not merely justifiable, but imperative upon honorable men, upon an honorable nation, where peace can only be obtained by the sacrifice of conscientious conviction or national welfare."[10] The burden of reshaping the minds of the youth in the village and beyond should not have been a task or responsibility placed on the shoulders of Kerkula and Uncle Nat alone but the shoulders of all adults, including parents, leaders of warring factions, and the government of Liberia, whom Theodore Roosevelt would have referred to as honorable men.

Unfortunately, parents voluntarily or involuntarily joined and recruited their children into the armed movements and conflicts. Additionally, there were parents and adults within communities who became the objects of disrespect, humiliation, intimidation, and torture by their children or other children within the community who carried guns or had the power to exercise unpunishable offenses. These parents and adults had no alternatives but to either obey orders and survive, flee their villages, take refuge on their farms, or join or support the movements.

---

9. Tzu, *Art of War*, 56.
10. Hoff, "Commentary: Presidential Quotes."

Being unaware of the youth's moral characters, the men embarked upon a three-part plan called "The Trinity Plan." The layout of the plan included church activities (male chorus and choir activities), recreation (sporting activities), and work (gold mining and local farming). Interestingly, this was not a plan that was documented. In other words, the plan was not written down on paper. They stored the plan mentally and closely monitored the progress made along the way. There were no stationeries available in the village or elsewhere to document their plan. Moreover, it was a risky idea to write things on paper for fear of being misconstrued as planning against the movements. It was also difficult to gather the village youth at a specific time and place to commence the planning. However, both men felt it expedient to solicit the participation of youth who were available for the planning and implementations of the plan.

Kerkula was mindful not to make any mistakes to keep a paper trail. He remembered his encounter with fighters a couple of years before when he had journeyed with three of his brothers from Division 45 to Kakata. Therefore, he advised his friend to eliminate any form of a paper trail to protect their plan. He was also suspicious that some of the youth who had expressed willingness to form part of the planning process could have been spies or youth on reconnaissance from the freedom fighter movement. They could have easily taken the information from the planning process back to whosoever needed it at the time, and things would have gone bad for both men.

You may wonder why it was that important to keep secret a simple plan of helping to reshape the minds of young people when there was nothing negative about it. One may argue there was a negative factor about the plan in the eyes of the warlords and others who committed their lives to the cause. These two men had embarked on reshaping the thought processes of young people who were the frontline soldiers of these militia groups. For the warlords and their movements, the idea to giving young people an opportunity to rethink their options amid a civil war threatened the fundamental formation, existence, and military strategies of the group themselves. They were not willing or prepared to tolerate a group or an idea that was contrary to their goals and objectives of seizing unconstitutional authority. Therefore, some leaders and ranking officials may have considered these initiatives by Kerkula and Uncle Nat as negative and dangerous to their successful operations. Though their plan may have been formulated and instituted on a small scale, it did not matter to warlords or fighters. Any and every attempt to change the minds of young people from supporting their cause and obeying orders was considered a threat that needed to be taken seriously and dealt with expeditiously.

The victories won by warring factions against each other, or their single most targeted opponent, the Armed Forces of Liberia (AFL), were not achieved by their individual or collective military strengths, weaponry or stockpile of the armory, or supernatural powers. They were also not won by their sophisticated and tactical guerilla fighting skills and maneuvering; neither were they won by the "powers of darkness." Instead, it was the consistent use and abuse of the youth who were conjured to willingly execute any or all orders given to them by their superiors even at the peril of their very lives or the lives of their parents, siblings, loved ones, relatives, and friends.

The youth were used as human shields and vehicles to speedily advance these attacks against their people despite the resistances they encountered along the way. They were the ones who bled and died the most. This is not to insinuate that adults did not bleed or die also; some lost their lives because of their involvement with certain warring factions, while others were sadly in the wrong places at the wrong times. Nevertheless, adults were mature enough to make conscientious and informed decisions about their willingness and unwillingness to join different movements. Unfortunately, the youth did not have the luxury to make informed decisions or decide what was best for them. It was the adults who decided for them in most cases.

THE IMPLEMENTATION OF THE TRINITY PLAN

As the Trinity Plan progressed, the implementation assignments were broken down into two parts. Kerkula led the plan on recreation, which included all sporting activities and the formation of the male chorus and church choir. He organized a male chorus with seven members, while Uncle Nat focused on the traditional Bassa choir's organization and management. The male chorus sang both traditional and English songs occasionally during Sunday worship services but mostly during moonlight sing inspirations or concerts in and out of the village.

On the other hand, the traditional church choir sang mostly in Bassa since it was spoken well by most of the members. A member of the youth group, H. Drobiah ("dro-biah"), who was mercifully gifted in singing traditional Bassa songs, led the dialect choir. He had the voice of a nightingale and a vocal sound as powerful as a trumpet. When he sang, the flapping sound of his voice echoed through the dark forest surrounding the village and could be heard as far as the banks of the St. John River. Villagers returning home from the farms could hear him sing and were always impressed and entertained. An African adage says, "The night has big ears and can hear the faintest sound." H. Drobiah's voice could be heard far and wide. He led the traditional choir to higher heights and encouraged more villagers to join.

The chorus entertained villagers with both English and traditional gospel music, sang in church during Sunday worship services, competed with other villages in gospel concerts and praise songs during moonlight events. Kerkula was also responsible for organizing two basketball teams to compete against each other mainly on weekends for entertainment purposes.

Meanwhile, Uncle Nat also led the plan on the church's administration restructuring, leadership development, evangelism, and work, which included gold mining and farming. He led the efforts to visit some of the gold mines during work hours and shared the gospel with the workers. It was apparent that not every worker or those doing business at the mines appreciated his periodic visits or teaching of the Holy Bible. Initially, many gold miners were not interested in listening to him. He did not blame those who hated him for preaching the good news. He knew some of them had not been allowed or not had the opportunity to hear the good news. Some made fun of him, but he seemed undeterred by their discontentment. He uncompromisingly visited the creeks each week when it came time to visit. Occasionally, Kerkula joined him during his weekly visits to the creeks when time permitted him to do so.

On the implementation plan for the church's activities, both men worked together simultaneously, assisting each other when help was needed.

As the days and weeks went by, more villagers began to return home early from their farms, and some took days off and stayed home when the choir and male chorus were scheduled to perform at night. More people were gathering during moonlight sing inspirations than during daytime activities. It was probably because the nighttime was cooler, relaxing, and shielded the identities of some of those attending who did not want to be seen or associated with churchgoers or Uncle Nat and Kerkula, who were referred to by some villagers and visitors as "church boys" or "choir boys."

The crowd gradually increased as the news about the nighttime activities spread throughout the towns and villages in the surrounding areas. More young boys and girls showed interest in all aspects of Uncle Nat and Kerkula's plan, and they started to invite their parents to join them. Parents attended the night events but did not stay longer like the youth, probably because of lack of interest or other engagements.

In some traditional Liberian villages, parents usually go to bed early because of their work schedules. They are usually engaged in long hours of hard labor farming, like felling trees, cutting down high forest and cleaning it up to prepare for planting season, hunting, trap making, fishing, and gathering food for their individual and respective families. Besides, traditional Liberian parents and their kids do not usually socialize or engage in the same activities for a longer period unless it is culturally mandated or necessary. For example, if a father and his son or a mother and her daughter were in the same societal group, a fishing club, a farming group (aka co-op), or a savings club, which is usually called a "Susu" in Liberia, they would eventually spend more time together especially during the hosting of such events. In some cases, the parents would be the ones directing the activities. Nevertheless, there are unique situations when the younger generation is placed in a leadership role above his adult parent. Such a situation is likely to occur when specific traditional arrangements have already been put in place or demanded by ancestral rites.

Unlike H. Drobiah, Kerkula did not have a nightingale's voice and could not sing any traditional songs. Remember, he was not from Kokoyah and had never spoken Bassa before. However, he always put forth his best efforts to learn the traditional songs, although he struggled to do so. He was not known for giving up a fight to achieve his goals so easily; neither was he a character who backed down or took no for an answer. He always knew what he wanted and sought the common good for those he worked with. The new friends he made in the village soon came to notice his steadfast character.

He spent time with H. Drobiah learning the words and meaning of the traditional songs that he taught the traditional choir. Soon, the songs began to make sense to him as he began to learn the meanings and how they applied to situations in life. He gradually fell in line with the rest of the choir members and began to sing in a new dialect as though he was born and raised in the village. He became intrigued by his newly spoken dialect. The excitement of knowing how successful he had become in singing songs in Bassa made him grow closer to H. Drobiah and appreciate the tribal group more. Visitors who saw him sing with the traditional choir during the moonlight sing inspirations thought he hailed from the village. Some did not know him personally. Others thought his parents were from the town or lived elsewhere and had returned home due to the civil unrest. Remember, Kokoyah has a multiethnic background with several tribes, including Bassa, Mano, Kpelle, and Gio. Kerkula was from the Kpelle tribe; he did not speak or understand any of the other dialects initially, but he later did.

Weeks went by, and the "Trinity Plan" began to impact the entire village. Words began to spread far and wide, and workers at the gold mines began to proudly sing the choir's traditional songs as they shoveled through the muddy dirt digging for gold. Some attempted to sing the songs of the male chorus but struggled to do so. They invited Kerkula to teach or sing for them when he visited the creeks with Uncle Nat. He willfully agreed to teach and sing for them with no reservations whatsoever. Many of the villagers who worked at the mines came to know him and made friends with him. Though he was new in town, it did not deter his willingness to engage those whom he interacted with. Some seemed to like him, while others vehemently displayed their dislike toward him and tried to scare him away, but they failed.

Soon, more miners on the other gold creeks in Dean's Town and residents of the surrounding villages heard about the male chorus and the traditional choir. They invited them to concerts and singing competitions during weekends. Both singing groups made several trips to nearby villages for concerts and attended worship services where they rendered special selections at the request of the church leaderships.

After several months of organizing both the male chorus and the traditional choir and teaching them how to work together as a team in glorifying God, it was time for both men to move on to the sports activities. The youth longed for a day when a different sport was brought to the village. This was evident by the kind of questions they asked about the sports they were about to practice and the enthusiasm each of them expressed when they heard it was basketball.

Before the introduction of basketball, soccer, which is a typical sport found in most Liberian urban or rural communities, was the only sport they had available to play. They had played it in and out of seasons for decades because no one seemed to have been interested in bringing another sport to town. Though they had an old basketball court in the village, no one had ever played on it for at least the past fifteen years. Therefore, Kerkula seized the opportunity to reintroduce basketball as a new sport since he could play it and knew most of the rules governing the game. He quickly formed two teams. There were no specific names given to each team. The teams bore the name of anyone available and willing to play during practices or on game day.

Unlike the moonlight sing inspirations, the basketball practices and games drew crowds of young people from in and around the village. Few elders stopped by when the boys were playing and did so unintentionally. Some elders had never seen a game where the players played with their hands rather than their feet like soccer. Not many people in the village were interested in or knew about the game of basketball. The youth who came out to practice or play the game did so to express a newly found talent that they had not discovered about themselves. Notwithstanding, few young people remained loyal to the teams. Kerkula quickly recognized their interest in the game and worked with them throughout his stay in the village.

With the level of successes achieved from sharing the good news of Jesus Christ with the gold miners, the male chorus, the introduction of basketball, and the moonlight sing inspirations, both men decided it was time to redirect their focus toward working directly with the church to increase awareness and membership and to convince the youth to become Christ-centered and not bearers of guns and other weapons. Unfortunately, no one, including Uncle Nat or Kerkula, saw it coming. They did not know working with a church, especially within a village setting, would have been the most daunting task ever. They soon came to find out it would become the hardest part of their implementation strategy.

Though the intensity of military hostilities in Liberia had subsided at some level, Liberians, especially the youth, were still battling with the aftermath of the period of civil unrest they had already experienced. The indelible imprints of warfare on the minds of the youth were still visible and are present today. There are hundreds of youths today in Liberia who are currently going through daily struggles for survival. Some have become destitute in their own country and have no sense of direction or purpose because their youth was stolen. Others have chosen other paths or the "quick way out" due to the country's current economic situation.

The voluntary or involuntary decisions which some youths made during three decades of civil unrest can be mostly attributed to their naivety and the abuse and marginalization they sustained at the hands of those who sought, used, and abused their innocence.

Their poor decision-making abilities have forced some of the youth to change their sexual orientation and have driven others deep into the dungeons of drug addiction, the oceans of crimes, and the dark pathways of illegal practices, which have led them into mental imprisonment, social isolation, educational and economic deprivation, and financial hardship. The evidence of these things is manifested in our society and can be found everywhere in Liberia today. No one needs to tell or show you the scars of fifteen years of brutal civil war. You only need to listen or look to see them.

Friedrich Nietzsche, a German philosopher, cultural critic, and preacher's son who popularized the phrase "God is dead," predicted that "when we find out that God has died in the 19th century, the 20th century will become the bloodiest century in history and universal madness will break out."[11] If his prediction is true, then the twentieth century was the bloodiest in human history. Therefore, we can arguably say that all of us, including our youth who actively participated in the civil war in Liberia, contributed in some ways to the realization of the twentieth century

---

11. Zacharias, "Universal Madness."

becoming the bloodiest century in history by the innocent lives that they took away individually or collectively.

Joseph Stalin once said, "One death is a tragedy; one million is a statistic."[12] We are responsible for creating unrealistic and unaccountable statistics by the deaths of our brothers and sisters whose lives were taken away on so-called battlefields, front lines, and in cold blood. All of us are responsible for not doing what was required of us individually or collectively as a people and country that could have prevented the senseless war and the deaths of so many. We can change the paths of history that will lead us in new directions for the betterment of ourselves, our people, and our country.

One way we can begin to reshape the course of history is to reshape the minds of our youth. Reshaping the minds of our youth is a national imperative and an ongoing process that has no end. If our society fails to continuously engage the youth and help reshape their mindset from what they were involved with to becoming useful citizens, it may lead Liberia into more future unrests, poor human resource development, and the lack of a true spirit of patriotism and nationalism. The choice is ours!

---

12. "Iosif Vissarionovich Dzhugashvili."

CHAPTER FIVE

Gold Mining

The earth is the LORD's, and everything in it, the world, and all who live in it; for he founded it on the seas and established it on the waters.

—PSALM 24:1-2, NIV

Gold mining can be an arduous process that requires continuous use of physical energy and alertness. One must frequently stay alert to avoid injury and seek ways to replenish lost energy supplies. However, gold mining can be easily manageable if miners have the technical skills and right equipment to do the work. For example, miners need to know how to prospect for gold and know which soil has gold and which does not. They also need to know about and observe safety measures when digging for gold. They need equipment like gold pans, metal detectors, mini sluice boxes, washing plants, blue bowls, soil scoops, or even front-end loaders. These skills and materials can help reduce the aches and pains sustained by strenuous and prolonged hours of physical labor that miners must exert daily to achieve a successful day's work and mining season.

For some of the local miners in Saye Wheh Town and other illegal miners within the nearby towns and villages, food, water, alcohol, and tobacco were often consumed and abused as energy busters to survive hard and long workdays. Other substances were used and abused to provide the needed energy to sustain them throughout the day.

Apart from the stress and aches that gold mining puts on the body, it brings many challenges to the environment or community—for example, pollution of air quality, watercourse contamination, landform degradation, and loss of biodiversity. There are also water bacteria and other land/water predators like poisonous snakes, frogs, leeches, and spiders, which are likely to be found in mining sites, can pose a danger, and often result in the death of a miner.

There are different processes in gold mining. Unfortunately, in third-world or developing countries like those in parts of Africa, for example, Liberia, Guinea, Sierra Leone, Ivory Coast, and others, illegal gold mining is more common. The pictures below depict illegal gold mining sites in several towns in the north, east, and west of Liberia, where illegal mining has become a way of life and a process by which villagers, young and old, can earn quick income.

Blemie in Zorgowee, Nimba County; Saye Wheh Town in Kokoyah, Bong County; and other towns in Grand Cape Mount County are in some of the counties in Liberia where illegal gold mining is prevalent. Gold miners in some of these areas do not have the luxury of using state-of-the-art equipment to make gold mining less stressful and less energy consuming. As a result of these illegal mining activities, the race to survive, or "survival of the fittest," often surpasses the respect for safety or the honor of human life.

Men, women, and children who work in these mines work with the mindset of not necessarily becoming rich but of earning a living that would enable them to put food on the tables of their families. They usually work quickly and faster with urgency and apprehension of being caught, which might eventually force them to lose the opportunity of earning a quick living. In some areas, individuals who are caught in illegal gold mining may face jail time or financial penalties but not necessarily in other areas, like Liberia and Sierra Leone.

It has been recorded that due to the lack of respect for safety and alertness during work hours, the rise in illegal arm carriers, the urgency, and fear of being caught in the process of illegal gold mining have resulted in the loss of many lives at mining sites. A story carried by *BBC News* on February 13, 2019, confirmed the deaths of five individuals who lost their lives to the collapse of illicit gold mines in Tappita, Nimba County, Liberia. According to the article, about thirty-five more people were still believed to have been missing after the gold pit walls collapsed. Interestingly, search and recovery efforts to find the missing individuals were done by the bare hands of other miners and sympathizers due to the lack of needed rescue equipment and personnel.[1]

---

1. Paye-Layleh, "Liberia Illicit Gold Mine Collapse."

In similar news reported in *FrontPage Africa* on July 11, 2020, over forty illegal gold miners were buried underground in Kartee Gold Mines located in Gboanipea, about ten kilometers away from Tappita, in District Number Six, Nimba County, Liberia. According to the article, the mines were ordered closed by mining authorities after the illegal miners' deaths. However, the order was later ignored, and mining activities resumed in the wake of the search to find the bodies of the missing miners.[2]

In a related story published by *Aljazeera* on May 6, 2020, a gold mine in Grand Cape Mount County in southwestern Liberia collapsed, leaving fifty or more people between the ages of twenty and twenty-eight years old dead.[3] These are clear indications of how dangerous illegal mining in Liberia and other developing countries has become. Time immemorial, the unfortunate deaths of illegal miners have occurred due to the lack of gold mining authorities' involvement and the establishment of comprehensive regulations that would discourage illegal mining and save local miners' lives. Indeed, what we love is killing and crippling us and what we desire is hunting our imaginations and destroying our ways of life.

GALAMSEY, A WAY OF LIFE

As strenuous as gold mining can be, miners in illegal mining areas find it inevitable and a way of making a quick living. A "quick living" means they can literally go to the gold mines and work couple of hours of hard labor and come home with few hundred dollars in local or foreign currencies, tax free in their pockets. Illegal mining is mostly referred to as "galamsey" in the West African subregion. The name is widely used mainly in Ghana. According to the *Oxford Advanced Learner's Dictionary*, "galamsey" is defined as small-scale illegal gold miners.[4] The term is derived from the phrase "gather them and sell." In Francophone or French-speaking nations, the term is also known as "Galamseyers" or "Orpailleurs."

2. Doloquee, "Breaking News: Liberia."
3. "Dozens Missing and Feared Dead."
4. "Galamsey."

Illegal gold mining site in Liberia

The picture seen above is an illegal mining site located in Dean's Town, one of few towns located closer to Saye Wheh Town in Kokoyah District, Bong County, Liberia. Miners at this mining site are engaged in local mining using gold washing pans and water buckets. They do not have sophisticated mining machinery or equipment. Such mining requires long hours of standing and bending over on one's feet in muddy infested water under a blazing and scorching sun.

Another illegal gold mining site in Kokoyah, Bong County, Liberia

The picture above shows a bigger mining site with more workers, including mothers and children working daily to earn a living. At such mining sites, the race to find gold-rich pockets or pits can often become controversial and brutal. Ownership or declaration of specific pits or digging sites must be made public or known to other miners to make a convincing claim. Even though the mines or gold creek as it is interchangeably called belongs to someone else, workers often fight amongst themselves for pieces of gold-rich land as though they owned the creeks.

Gold mining sites in the hills

This mining site above is one of several sites in Nimba County. In this area, gold miners often describe such a site as "death trap" because of the hills and the chances of the walls breaking down on miners while at work. Often when this occurs, the result is the death of a miner.

Interestingly, some miners prefer to work on hilly sites because of the quality of gold (e.g., big and bright nuggets) found in these areas. They also prefer the hill because it is on dry grounds and not in the swamp where the chances of contracting bacterial infections or other diseases are common or most likely to occur.

The next mining site below is in Blemie, Zorgowee, Nimba County, Liberia. This site is among the easier mining areas because it is mostly on flat sandy grounds with less bush or grass. Miners in this area do not have the challenge of digging deeper or harder to reach the gold-rich gravel. They do not have to fear the collapse of the walls or "death traps" like those on the hilly sites. However, this mining area is among some of the sites where contracting bacterial infections or being bitten by predators like snakes, leeches, and spiders are most likely. There are lots of still waters that can become breeding grounds for mosquitoes and other diseases.

One of several sandy gold mines in Zorgowee, Nimba County

This is another gold mining site in Blemie, Zorgowee, Nimba County, Liberia. The mine is in the northeastern part of the town. This site is like mining creeks in Saye Wheh Town and other surrounding villages.

Another mining site in Blemie, Zorgowee

The picture above is another view of a mining site in Blemie, Zorgowee, Nimba County, Liberia. This mine is also like some mining sites in Saye Wheh Town.

Historically, gold and diamond mining in Liberia were carried out largely by alluvial mining of small-scale operations. It is estimated that there have been over one hundred thousand artisanal miners in Liberia. It is also estimated that Liberia currently has a reserve of gold amounting to three million ounces. Gold is responsible for the development of a good percentage of Liberia's economy. Apart from illegal miners' activities, gold mining across Liberia has created more jobs for Liberians and foreign investors.

You may be wondering by now why the subject of gold mining is relevant to the writing of this book or what gold mining has to do with Kerkula and Uncle Nat living in Saye Wheh Town. Well, you will realize that I spent much time informing you about unfortunate incidents on different mining sites in Liberia where illegal mining resulted in the deaths of ordinary miners who sought survival by risking their lives. The discussion of illegal mining activities is essential in writing this book for many reasons.

The gold mines and those who worked in the fields during the civil war became a good platform for extending the church's activities in Saye Wheh Town to other towns and villages. The miners played significant roles in the expansion and implementation of the "Trinity Plan." They also helped in evangelism and outreach, especially to other miners, local merchants, and visitors they interacted with. They became the "silent salesmen" or "silent voices" that Kerkula and Uncle Nat needed to move the message about youth activities to other young people in nearby towns and villages.

Gathering at the gold mines also made it easier for villagers young and old to hear the good news of Jesus Christ through songs, even when they were not interested in listening to uncle Nat or to hear Kerkula sing along with the other miners. The mines created opportunities for Kerkula and Uncle Nat to generate personal income and funds needed to support the church and youth's projects.

Working at the creeks with miners allowed both men to discover their strengths and weaknesses in evangelism and outreach from the challenges and threats they encountered individually and collectively. Though these developments helped improve the church's capacity to witness more, it also brought awareness to the town and became a pivotal moment in the two men's lives. It was the first time in their friendship for both men to work together on a church-related project away from their home church in Bong Mines.

In chapter 4, I discussed the topic of "reshaping the minds of the youth amid a civil war." For a minute, imagine the level of challenges and setbacks one may have likely encountered while trying to convince a person, especially an adult who has his or her mind made up or fixed on a way of life. Imagine what it would take for him or her to neglect the survival strategies and depend on the words and works of an invisible God rather than the benefits of a physical object (gold), which can bring him or her instant wealth. Honestly, it is not an easy task if you must do it by your efforts. It takes the power of God to make one successful in achieving such an undertaking. It is often said that "a race is a man running alone, but Grace is when God runs with him."[5]

Another reason why the discussion of the gold mines is relevant to this book is that some of the individuals who lived in and around the village and worked in those mines are still alive today and probably involved with the church in Saye Wheh Town. It would bestow pride and honor upon them and their families to know that their decisions to rely on the word of God and endure hardship during the civil war and not the temporary riches acquired from gold mining did not go unnoticed. It would also make them realize that their desires for becoming members of the youth group and the church were not taken for granted or forgotten. Instead, they would come to believe God kept his promise to his word and rewarded their faithfulness and commitments. It would also give them a reason to believe and continue to trust in the faith shared with them by Kerkula and Uncle Nat.

MYTHS ABOUT GOLD MINING IN SAYE WHEH TOWN/LIBERIA

There are many myths about gold mining in Liberia. Saye Wheh Town is one of several mining towns in Liberia where illegal miners hold certain myths to be self-evident that the presence of gold in the creeks is not by divine provision but given by the power of the gods of their ancestors. Therefore, they must obey the gods' will and powers to receive more gold annually in the creeks. Among the myths that many miners hold sacred, here are a few that are most common amongst those we visited or worked with.

- *The sacrifice of a white chicken or sheep*

Some miners believe that a sacrifice of a white chicken or a ram in the gold mines will appease the so-called "gods of gold" and cause them to release more gold in the mines. Therefore, the gold mines owners would purchase either a white chicken or a ram and select a day on which most miners would be available to assemble at the mines for the sacrifice to be carried out. Interestingly, it is assumed that the bigger the price, the better the outcome. In this case, a sheep sacrifice would produce a bigger and better outcome than a chicken. Therefore, a sheep sacrifice would most likely be made instead of a chicken sacrifice.

---

5. https://www.pinterest.com/pin/7851041475119937213/.

After everyone has assembled at the mines for the sacrifice ceremony, a ritual will be performed by an elder who is preferably a witch doctor. The token or sacrificed animal (white chicken or ram) will be let loose alive on the mines and allowed to live the rest of its life freely throughout the mines as long as it remains open. It is forbidden per the ritual that the sacrificed animal be caught or killed by anyone. It is believed that whosoever catches and kills the token or sacrificed animal will eventually die.

- *The sacrifice of a human life*

This is one of the most sacred but less talked about myths on the gold mines. Some miners believe when the walls of a mine or gold pit fall, and miners are trapped and killed, it is a preplanned sacrifice intended to please the gods. Some believe no incident occurs in the mines which results in a miner's death that is not preplanned. They have a common name to describe the incident. They refer to it as the "breaking of a shovel." In other words, when a miner is trapped and killed, it means a shovel has been broken. It is assumed that the death of a person in the mines triggers more gold than any other sacrifice made by the mine owners. They believe human blood sacrifice is worth more to the gods (aka Genies) than any animal's blood or other sacrifices.

- *The gold in the ground is produced and given by gods or genies.*

Owners of mining creeks and ordinary miners do not believe that the gold in the mines was brought there naturally by the creator of the universe. They believe that gold belongs to the gods of their ancestors, and to obtain more from them one must appease and appreciate them by providing what they have requested, regardless of the price one must pay. Mine owners believe without giving the gods or genies what they request, a mining creek cannot become productive. In contrast to this view, Psalm 24:1 says, "The earth is the Lord's, and everything in it, the world and all who live in it." I am not sure if mine owners or workers are familiar with this Scripture and its connection to minerals in the earth.

- *You must be an alcoholic or chain smoker to become a gold digger or miner.*

It is widely believed by a good percentage of illegal gold miners that to withstand the hard labor, scorching heat from the sub-Saharan sun, cold, muddy, dirty, and swampy water, along with the bodily aches and pain miners experienced daily, one has to consume lots of alcoholic beverages, smoke heavily, or use other narcotics. This is a myth and not a fact. Some miners were careful and worked smarter and did not have to engage in any wrong health practices to become gold miners. Some of the miners who did not engage in those practices succeeded simply by observing safety measures, adhering to minimum health precautions, and following self-guided nutrition practices. They also ate healthily, working a few hours in the day, and had enough sleep at night before resuming work the next day.

On the contrary, some miners engaged in these practices either as a way of escape for their unproductive work ethic or to "fit in" with the other miners who were also engaged in similar practices.

- *To succeed and become rich from gold mining, one must engage in dishonest practices.*

Illegal miners consider dishonesty a way of life and cheating as a game of chase or hide and seek. In other words, if a miner is clever enough to outsmart his coworkers or mine owner by cheating and being dishonest without being caught in the act, he or she has mastered gold mining. This means he or she is surely going to succeed financially. They do not consider these dishonest practices as crimes committed against the mine owners, coworkers, or mining authorities. It is the very reason why they are called "illegal miners." They disregard regulations from mining authorities but pretend as though they honor them and steal a portion of the entire gold accumulated at the end of a day's work. Most often, stealing gold is done amongst miners when washing the gravel or refining the gold. Egoism or self-centeredness are prime words for illegal gold mining. An illegal gold miner wants the gold for himself and not the creek owner.

Illegal miners would do anything and everything to protect their territorial workspace and the gold that was extracted from it. Violence may often erupt between miners when a conflict of interest like a fight for a better mining site or pit occurs. Smaller work teams of miners are formed for several reasons but mostly to ensure collaborative efforts and to effectively use their energy, build allegiance to each other, increase workspace to create better opportunities to extract more gold promptly, and consolidate efforts to intimidate and drive away independent and weaker workers to gain their workspaces. This is expected and has become an acceptable norm on most mining sites in Saye Wheh Town. One may consider this a "survival of the fittest."

CHAPTER SIX

Evil in the Heart of a God-Fearing Man

The heart is deceitful above all things, and desperately wicked: who can know it?

—JEREMIAH 17:9

IF CHRISTIANITY IS TRULY having a relationship with Jesus Christ and godliness an act of obeying the laws of the Almighty God, how possible is it for evil to exist in the heart of a God-fearing person? How can a person who holds a spiritual position in the church, teaches the Bible, and portrays a dedicated Christian life conforms to a life of evil? How can a person who has become a role model for non-Christians live a double life as a Christian and a witch? These are questions that seem difficult to answer, especially by young Christians—those who are not mature in the faith, and maybe those who have declared their intentions for the first time to become Christians. Indeed, evil is perfected and perpetuated if we fail to recognize and honor God's purpose for our lives.

In this chapter, the author tries to answer these questions by briefly discussing some of the activities of a man who was once thought to be a dedicated Christian until his double lives were exposed. To discuss these issues, we must first consider the definition of the heart and what it means for it to conceive evil. Biologically, the heart is defined as the chambered muscular organ of vertebrates that moves blood through the body by repeated, rhythmic contractions. Spiritually, the heart is a special part of the human body out of it spring the issues of life (Prov 4:23); it is deceitful above all things and desperately wicked (Jer 17:9–10).

The conception or desire to harbor evil in one's heart is a matter of choice and not necessarily a compulsion or demand made by one person to another. Even though there are times when evil is committed because of others' influence, an individual must be willing and convinced to partake in evil. Committing or engaging in any form of evil for the most part is intentional and not a mistake. When evil is conceived, it is the outcome of whatever plan that had been carried out which brings satisfaction to the perpetrator. The personal hurts and miseries of the victim are not considered important by the one inflating the pain. Instead, it is the exact outcome which the perpetrator envisions before he or she goes out to implement the plan to commit evil. This is one reason why God detests evil and punishes the perpetrator. Therefore, in this chapter, the discussion of "evil in the heart of a God-fearing man" will focus mainly on the spiritual nature of a man's heart.

There are many definitions and interpretations of what it means to be a "God-fearing" man or person. Dr. David Jeremiah, senior pastor of Shadow Mountain Community Church in San Diego, California, USA, and founder of Turning Point International Ministry defines godliness or the act of being God-fearing simply as living a faithful and obedient Christian life.[1] He believes godliness is one of seven qualities that all Christians are instructed to add to their faith after becoming saved.

A misconception of godliness or what it means to be a "God-fearing" man or person exists when the cultural, traditional, and societal beliefs of a person or group of people that are inconsistent with God's word are used as foundational truths and premises to justify the behaviors of churchgoers or so-called Christians. As such, the true meaning of a "God-fearing" man or person may sometimes become misinterpreted and subjected to an individual's perception and understanding of how his or her culture, tradition, and society define it.

No one would have thought or said out loud that Deacon J, or Uncle J as he was often referred to, was living a double life. He was a quiet and highly respected individual by most villagers and residents of Saye Wheh Town. He was approximately 5'8" tall, dark in complexion, and wore a bit of an afro on his head. He maintained no facial hair and always kept an honest look on his face. He was well-shaven and dressed modestly each day at work, church, or during his leisure time in the village. Like many other villagers, he farmed and made a living by occasionally working in the

---

1. Jeremiah, "What Is Godliness?"

gold mines. He was not fond of digging gold or hanging around the gold creeks. He was mostly involved with farming activities and performed his role as head deacon of the local church. Some church members, including Kerkula and Uncle Nat, who became members shortly upon arrival in the town, regarded him as a role model and a spiritually minded individual. As a head deacon and founding member, he exercised spiritual authority during church meetings and activities.

There was a certain persona about him, which seemed to, unfortunately, repel some young people away. Young people saw him as being "super-spiritual," meaning he always considered himself perfect and took spirituality to a different level. Additionally, others believed he was too straightforward in dealing with church members about doctrinal issues and rendered condemnations on villagers and other residents who were not affiliated or involved with the church's activities. Some villagers thought he lacked people skills and the ability to engage or peacefully coexist with others, which forced some of them to stay away from him. His presence, authority, and quiet nature were recognized and felt every time he entered a room, but his likeability was equal to his absence. Almost everyone knew this about him, including visitors and other business people who came through the village. He kept a smile on his face when he approached a fellow villager or visitor, which some considered a fake attitude because he usually wore a frown on his face when he was alone or interacting with others, especially church members.

Upon the arrival of Uncle Nat, Kerkula, and the other two individuals to Saye Wheh Town, the church took the initiative to make housing accommodations for the other three individuals, excluding Uncle Nat since it was his hometown. Kerkula and J. Yarsiah, the other youth with them, shared a room while the girl had a room to herself. Uncle Nat stayed in his brother's house since there was not enough room to accommodate everyone.

Several months passed, and the church decided to relocate Kerkula and J. Yarsiah since their landlord had increased the rent, which the boys could not afford because they were not working to generate income. The girl was moved into the pastor's house because her safety and welfare became imperative.

According to the information Kerkula received, Deacon J had volunteered to become their host parent for the rest of their stay in the village since they could no longer stay at the house they had rented. Kerkula and J. Yarsiah moved into Deacon J family's home a few days after the decision was reached.

LIVING WITH DEACON J AND FAMILY

Deacon J lived with his mother and another individual in a four-bedroom house. The house was painted white and had zinc roofing with wooden windows. It was located a few yards from the church and situated on top of a small hill that overlooked the gravel road that led to a nearby village. There was a grave underneath a cola-nut tree, which Deacon J and his mom often sat on during hot, sunny days. The grave was said to be his grandfather's, his mother's father. Kerkula and J. Yarsiah were given a small room within the house. The room was approximately ten by ten feet. There was no ceiling or a bed in the room for both individuals to sleep on. Initially, both boys used a bamboo mat, which Yarsiah platted himself. He was good at making traditional arts and crafts. Several months after the boys moved in, they purchased a small foam mattress with the money they raised from digging gold.

Like most traditional village houses and huts, the walls in the rooms and around the house were rubbed down with mud and whitewash, a white clay substance that the villagers usually dig from the swamp or muddy areas. The white clay is turned into a liquid-like substance and used to paint their homes. Some villagers would add colorings to the white clay substance to give it different colors and shades.

Unlike Kerkula, Yarsiah was good at speaking the Kpelle dialect and knew more about its culture and traditions. He could survive easily in any village community. He was also a member of the traditional Poro Society, which gave him leverage over the others when it came time to interact with the traditionalists or when the Kpelle Country Devil visited the village.

For the most part, both men enjoyed their stay at Deacon J and his mom's home. Some afternoons when both men and Uncle J did not go to work, they would sit together in the backyard under the cola-nut tree next to his grandfather's grave and have lengthy conversations about every subject. They would talk about the church and its role in the community, their families, the civil war, its challenges, and traditional issues. Deacon J did not talk openly about the war or politics in general. He was very mindful of expressing his opinion about the war or politics to Kerkula, J. Yarsiah, or residents in the town. He would rather talk about church or traditional issues one-on-one with individuals than in a group environment. However, he was an assertive individual and always portrayed himself as knowledgeable even when he did not have much to contribute to a discussion or knew what was being discussed. It seemed the fear of rejection or underestimation by others always compelled him to exhibit pretentious behaviors.

Several months passed by; both men and Uncle J continued to work on their bonding and working together in the church. Some villagers began to see and acknowledge the evidence of the friendship between the boys and Uncle J. They began to call them Deacon J's sons. The boys did not mind being called Uncle J's children. They loved, trusted, and respected him for who he was and his role in the church. He spoke a little bit of Kpelle, and because of that, Kerkula and the others, including the girl, M. Brown, appreciated and drew closer to him. They became closer and confided in him their plans to work harder, leave Saye Wheh Town, and return home to Bong Mines someday. No one else knew their plan but he and Uncle Nat.

One early Thursday morning, Kerkula woke up feeling a sharp and unusual pain in his left ear. At first, the pain became a little troubling but suddenly went away. After a while, the pain returned but more severe, this time leaving him in total discomfort. He rolled on the bare floor of their bedroom in agony for a while, but the pain never went away. It became even more severe and so discomforting that he could not sit or lay in one position for more than a minute. He was alone in their bedroom. It seemed no one was around to see or hear him struggling through his pain. However, Uncle J, his mom, and another older gentleman who also lived in the house were home on the morning of the incident, but no one came out to help him. J. Yarsiah was not home; he had gone down the hill to have talks with Uncle Nat and M. Brown. He had left the room early because he felt Kerkula was tired and needed some time to sleep and rest his body since he had worked longer and harder on two consecutive days at the gold mines.

As the pain level intensified, Kerkula cried even more for help, but no one came out to assist him. By this time, there were no cellphones or means of communication Kerkula could have used to reach his friends. As the sun began to rise, Yarsiah returned to the room and found Kerkula crying of pain.

"What is going on?" Yarsiah asked.

"I don't know what is happening to me. My left ear is hurting severely," Kerkula replied.

"Did you hit your head against something, or did someone hit your ear?" Yarsiah asked. "Did something mistakenly go into your ear?" Yarsiah asked his friend repeatedly, "Has anyone come in here to see you? Did you call Uncle J?"

"No one has been here to see me. Yes, I called Uncle J, but he has not come yet," Kerkula replied.

By this time, Yarsiah was becoming more concerned and seemed to have been a little worried and bemused about his friend's condition. He paced back and forth in the room, perplexed and unsettled. Finally, he ran out of the room as though he had found the solution to his friend's painful ear.

"Where are you going now?" Kerkula asked tearfully as his speech became slurred as though he was chuckling.

"I am going to call Uncle Nat," Yarsiah replied. "I will be right back, don't worry."

He left his friend alone in their room and ran as fast as he could to inform Uncle Nat and M. Brown about what had happened. Immediately after Uncle Nat received the message, he ran up the hill to find Kerkula in their room.

"Young man, what is going on with you?" Uncle Nat asked.

"GAP, I am not sure what is happing to me," Kerkula responded. (Both men often called each other nicknames as they found fit. Uncle Nat was fond of calling Kerkula "young man" occasionally during church activities because he had heard Kerkula's father repeatedly calling young boys who lived in their neighborhood "young men." On the other hand, Kerkula was comfortable calling Uncle Nat "GAP" because it was an acronym that he, Uncle Nat, introduced at a youth Bible study, which stood for "God Answers Prayers.")

The conversations went on between the two men for a few minutes while Kerkula struggled with the pain in his ear. Uncle Nat was mystified and did not know what to conclude about his friend's situation. At first, he thought it was an ordinary pain he was experiencing which could have easily been remedied by Kerkula simply consuming a couple of painkiller medications like Tylenol, Ibuprofen, Motrin, Aspirin, or other traditional herbs. Little did he know that what his friend was experiencing was more than just an ordinary ear pain. He soon realized that something had to be done quickly to help with Kerkula's situation, or else he would have to spend the entire night in agony. Uncle Nat was also concerned that none of the house residents, including Deacon J, was with Kerkula or had informed him about the situation. He found their actions toward Kerkula somewhat surprising and disturbing. He was under the impression that Deacon J and his family would do everything to care for Kerkula and J. Yarsiah because they were Christians. Moreover, they willfully volunteered to host the two boys after they could no longer stay at their first location.

THE HERBALIST

There were no clinics or medical facilities in the village. Villagers who sought medical treatments and other forms of healthcare assistance had to walk by foot to the district headquarters of Botota. There was a family in town who had some nursing experience. Two of the sons within this family were Licensed Practical Nurses (LPNs). Unfortunately, both men had traveled away, and their return to the village was not known. There was also a local shop that sold dry goods and had a small portion of medications for sale. Interestingly, both the owner and his friend who ran the shop were out of town as well. One of the friends had gone to Gbarnga to purchase new supplies of medications while the other had gone to transact business as usual in Danané, the Ivory Coast.

The absence of medications and medical help in the village to remedy Kerkula's situation forced both Uncle Nat and Yarsiah to think outside the box. They first decided to seek medical assistance in another village. They thought taking Kerkula to Botota, which was several miles away from Saye Wheh Town, was their best option to get immediate medical care. However, after consultations with a few elders in the town, the name of an older gentleman—an herbalist who believed in the science of traditional medicine and practiced it well, based on his records, was recommended to them. Some of the elders in the town and surrounding villages thought highly of him. They believed he was good at helping individuals with multiple symptoms and illnesses. Hence, they were convinced he could help stop Kerkula's pain. However, he lived in Gbohn's ("gbooh") Town, a small village approximately ten kilometers away from Saye Wheh Town. They had to take Kerkula to meet the older man if he was going to help him.

Unfortunately, there was no available means of transportation to take Kerkula and the others to see the herbalist. The older man lived in a small village with no car roads but a few huts and mud houses. To get to his village, they had to walk on foot for approximately three or more hours through narrow paths and cold streams.

As the sun rose, Uncle Nat became more concerned that time was not on their side, and they needed to leave town to make it to the older man's village before night fell. He looked at his friend and realized that he was becoming more discomforted and could no longer bear the pain he was experiencing.

He stretched out his right hand down toward his friend, picked him up from the floor, and asked him to get on his back. At first, Kerkula was confused about what his friend was asking him to do. He had a bizarre look on his face as he stared upwards directly into his friend's face. "Get on my back." Uncle Nat said. "We have to find a way to get to the old man before it gets late. There are no other means of transportation available to us at this time other than carrying you on my back." Kerkula hopped on his friend's back, as Uncle Nat was in a position of readiness to take him to see the older man.

During the transition from the floor to his friend's back, Uncle J and his mom stopped by at the boy's room and asked what was going on. Uncle Nat informed them about the situation, but they did not seem bothered by the information they had received. Both individuals and other onlookers stood aside and watched Uncle Nat struggled with removing his friend from their room and getting started on their journey.

Uncle Nat was not alone in taking Kerkula to his medical treatment. He was accompanied by Yarsiah and another female who later became introduced as Kerkula's friend. She was the daughter of a prominent mother of Saye Wheh Town, whose father was the village's founder. It later became known that this girl became romantically involved with Kerkula and the mother of his two children a couple of years after they left the village and traveled out of the country.

They traveled several miles on foot in the hot sun and the cool shades of tall trees and wild bushes before reaching the village. They made several stops along the way to take brief rests and get food to eat and water to drink. Uncle Nat and J. Yarsiah also took turns carrying Kerkula. After approximately three and a half hours of walking, they finally reached the village of the older man. Upon arrival, they noticed that the older man was in his room. He lived in a small mud hut, which is typical in most villages in Liberia. His hut was in the northern part of a small village called Gbohn's Town. The town was comprised of few huts and houses at the time.

He came out of his hut, made a formal traditional greeting in Bassa, and encouraged his guests to be seated. Unfortunately, there were not enough seats to accommodate all three of them. Therefore, he quickly started his conversation with them to allow enough time for them to return home after he was done providing the help Kerkula needed.

He spoke in Bassa with a tender voice and paused several times in his speech as though he were finished talking. Each time he paused, he started right back up again after a couple of minutes. It was apparent that he did not speak English. He never attempted to speak it throughout his time with his guests. His long narration and idiosyncratic deposition about his expertise with herbs made Kerkula question his ability to provide the right medicine and treatment that would have eventually helped ease his pain.

He looked at his friends with a sense of doubt and trepidation of the unknown. He hoped they could seek help in another village and not with the older man because of the things he had said. Uncle Nat paid his friend no mind because he did not think the older man had said or done anything fearful or threatening. He thought Kerkula was becoming confused about what the older man had said because he did not understand Bassa. He wrongly perceived the older man was talking negatively about him and that he did not know much about herbs.

The older man excused himself after a long talk in Bassa with Uncle Nat. He went behind his hut and disappeared suddenly among the banana orchard and orange trees. He stayed away for approximately twenty minutes before returning. Upon his return, they noticed him chewing on something but did not know exactly what it was. They soon found out after he spoke with Uncle Nat that he was chewing on the herbs he had gone to get to treat Kerkula.

"Gboweh, have him sit here." The older man commanded Uncle Nat to tell his friend.

"Move closer, Kerkula," Uncle Nat asked his friend.

"What is he about to do, and where is the medicine?" Kerkula asked.

"I am not sure; let's wait and see what the old man is going to do," Uncle Nat replied.

"Something is not right! Something is just not right!" Kerkula lamented.

"Well, let's not be too judgmental, Kerkula," Uncle Nat cautioned his friend. "Let's give the old man a chance. Maybe his expertise is just what we might need."

"Hopefully, I have not given you any reasons to suggest that I am judgmental in what I have said. I just believe something is just not right with this entire process," Kerkula spoke emphatically.

"I totally understand your position but let us give the old man a chance to do what he is about to do. Maybe it might just be the help that we need," Uncle Nat told his friend.

The older man moved Kerkula's head backward and sideways. He pulled his earlobe downwards and positioned his mouth in it. He deposited a greenish liquid content of what was in his mouth into Kerkula's left ear and asked him to sit in the corner of the porch with his ear slanted towards his right shoulder. The pain gradually subsided from Kerkula's ear a couple of minutes later after the older man deposited the liquid substance. Unfortunately, the pain did not go away completely. Kerkula felt a little bit of relief, which was better than the initial pain level he had experience prior to coming over to the old man's hut.

At first, everyone seemed happy when the pain subsided. They believed Kerkula was finally healed. They decided to compensate the old man for his good work and return to Saye Wheh Town the same evening. Suddenly, after an hour of quietness, Kerkula's pain returned but more severe than before. He began to cry out loud and fell to the ground several times in agony. No doubt, he was in pain and struggling with another setback.

THE TRIP TO BOTOTA

Uncle Nat made a quick decision without Kerkula's consent to take him to Botota immediately to seek additional medical treatment. He figured that there would have been no hope for Kerkula to receive medical treatment if they had returned to Saye Wheh Town or stayed with the old man to continue his treatment. He compensated and thanked the old man for his kind gesture toward them and bid him goodbye.

They got back on the road and headed toward Botota, walking for approximately two and a half hours more. After an exhausting walk in the sun taking turns carrying Kerkula on their backs, they reached Botota during the evening hours. No doubt, it was clear that the three friends including Kerkula were hungry for food and needed water to drink. They had not consumed any solid food or had a drink of water throughout the journey to the old man or Botota apart from wild berries and fruits they had picked from the floor of the forest and eaten.

Upon arrival in Botota, the town looked a little crowded and busy. There were movements of people and vehicles everywhere. There were pickup trucks full of rebel fighters driving back and forth. It was the first time in days that Kerkula and the others had come face to face with a good number of freedom fighters in the streets. They kept driving from one corner of the town to their main office. Unlike Gbohn's Town, Botota was much larger and had gravel roads throughout the town. There were many decent houses and a medical facility located along a hillside.

Usually on weekends, especially Saturdays, most villages and local towns are crowded with residents and visitors who find time to relax or engage in family fun activities away from a long week of tedious farming or gold mining. This could have been one good reason why, upon arrival, the town was crowded and busy.

Their first stop was at the clinic, the only medical facility in town. Unfortunately, it was closed for the day. There were workers at the facility who informed Uncle Nat that all medical personnel had left for the day, and the on-call nurse had not reported to duty yet. The worker informed Uncle Nat and the others that the on-call nurse usually started his or her shift at 7:00 p.m. and ended at 7:00 a.m. the next day. There was no one else at the facility to handle medical issues but the security and janitor, who were found closing the building. Fortunately, another worker who happened to still be in the building came out to where they were standing. He saw the anguish on Kerkula's face and directed them to the home of the on-call nurse, who lived close by the clinic. They hurried to his house to find him. He had just returned from taking a bath and was getting prepared for the evening shift at the clinic.

"Good evening sir, my name is Nat, and these are my friends." Uncle Nat introduced his friends to the nurse. "We were directed to come and see you for some medical assistance for our friend," Uncle Nat said.

"How can I help you?" the nurse replied.

"Our friend and brother is not feeling well. He has a severe ear infection, which has bothered him for the past few days," Uncle Nat said. "We brought him to see an old man in Gbohn's town, but he could not help him. Therefore, we decided to come over here. Can you help us please?" Uncle Nat asked.

"What is it you would like me to do?" the nurse asked as though he had not seen how uneasy Kerkula looked.

"We would like for you to kindly help treat our friend. He is in severe pain and needs help immediately," Uncle Nat said.

"Take him in the third room to your left down this hallway, and I will be with you in few minutes," the nurse said.

They took him to the room as requested by the on-call nurse. After a few minutes of waiting in the room, the nurse returned wearing a white scrub with a first-aid kit in his right hand. There were several medical supplies in the kit, including syringes, Cottle columella clamps, Shapleigh ear curette, McCabe facial nerve dissector, band-aids, bandages, isopropyl rubbing alcohol, etc. Uncle Nat and the others were surprised to see how prepared and ready the nurse was to treat their friend. It had been difficult during the civil war to find medical supplies in such quantity and in such a remote village. Most of the local clinics in cities and bigger towns were either closed down, out of medical supplies due to no additional supplies coming in, overwhelmed by the influx of wounded fighters and displaced people, or stopped by the mere fact that the limited supplies in these areas had either been looted, stored away for personal use, or confiscated by those in authority and moved to other locations. Though Botota is a district headquarter, it is not one of those larger cities in the country that would guarantee the availability of good medical treatment, services, and supplies.

The nurse examined Kerkula's ear and said, "He will have to be put on antibiotic injections for a couple of days to be fully healed. Unfortunately, he will have to stay in town to complete four days of treatment since only the clinic and not I have antibiotic pills to send him home with today." He did not say exactly what had happened to Kerkula's ear, but he emphasized that he needed to put him on antibiotic injections immediately to save his ear.

The possibility of Kerkula receiving full medical treatment in Botota felt good and provided a sense of relief to his friends. However, keeping him in town for four days became another stressor that Uncle Nat and the other had to contend with. They did not know anyone in town they could stay with. Also, there were no motels or hotels where they could seek accommodations for the four days. The only option they had was to abandon the treatment and return to Saye Wheh Town or negotiate with the nurse to provide accommodation for them.

Uncle Nat was hesitant to ask the nurse to accommodate them for the four nights since he had already generously agreed to treat his friend. He felt it would have been too much to ask of one person. However, realizing that they had no other choice that would have guaranteed Kerkula's treatment and because the night was falling quickly, he mustered the courage to go and speak with the nurse.

As they struggled to compose themselves, the nurse overheard their conversations in the other room and walked up to them. "Kerkula may stay in this room with one other person for the length of his treatment, but two of you will have to return to your village. There are not enough rooms in this house to accommodate all of you at the same time. Moreover, I do not want my family and me to be put under surveillance by the freedom fighters. Having too many strangers at one time in the same house may raise a red flag with the freedom fighters, which may have unpredictable consequences. I am afraid that is not what I would like for my family and me at this time. Therefore, I will only provide accommodation for the two of you."

The nurse spoke about his skepticism and fear of the freedom fighters as though Kerkula and the other had no experience with these things or as though they had not lived in rebel-controlled territories and known the activities of the fighters.

As usual, Uncle Nat was troubled but not broken. He knew leaving town that evening to return to Saye Wheh Town would have been an uncalculated risk to take. He also knew that being in town with nowhere to stay for the night was becoming a challenge, and he and the others needed to act quickly before it was too late. Throughout the planning and negotiations, Kerkula was not fully involved because he was not feeling well. The nurse had already administered the first dose of antibiotic injection and other medications to him and they started to impact his alertness. He gradually fell asleep as the medications began to take effect. His subconscious mind could not remember what had happened to his friends because he had fallen into a deep sleep.

Uncle Nat made another quick decision and reached out once again to the nurse. He asked if he could allow all of them to spend the night together with Kerkula to make sure that all was well with him before leaving the next morning. Without any hesitations, the nurse consented and provided them with additional room and some food to eat. He asked his wife to fetch bath water for each of his guests, beginning with the girl. He offered them more bedding and sleeping materials for the night. He bid them goodnight and walked away to his bedroom, which was on the other side of the living room. He stayed in his room for couple of minutes before going to work at the clinic.

The night came and passed by quickly. The next morning, they were greeted by the nurse dressed up beautifully in his medical scrubs and on his way back to work. Apparently, there was a need for his services at the clinic. He had worked all night, came home, took a shower, and was heading right back out of his home to the clinic.

He quickly administered another dose of antibiotic injection and gave Kerkula a couple of pain pills. "I am headed to the clinic. By noon, you and your friends should come up and see me," the nurse requested. "I am hoping to get some medications for you to take home today. With the medications and injections, you have already received, your treatment will be complete, and you should be able to leave this evening with your friends."

The nurse's statements brought some relief to Uncle Nat and excitement to the others, including Kerkula, who felt much better after receiving his first sets of treatments. He was sitting upright and spent time walking around the room. He had already received four antibiotic injections and some pain medications, and he was responding well to the treatments.

They visited the clinic and met with the nurse per his request. He gave Kerkula his afternoon injection and a parcel of medications to take with him to Saye Wheh Town. He asked them to return to his house and wait for him. He arrived a couple of hours later and had dinner with them. He encouraged them to spend the night since it was almost night, and they agreed.

By this time, a mutual friendship had developed among them. The nurse had become more comfortable with everyone else and especially Kerkula, his patient. He spoke Bassa, Kpelle, and English well but chose to communicate in English rather than dialects since everyone could understand and speak it.

Everyone seemed to have had a good time. Kerkula was glad that he had finally received the treatment he longed for and felt much better day after day. They spent the night together sitting in the moonlight in front of the nurse's home till about midnight before going to bed. The night went well with no problems and less pain in Kerkula's ear.

The next morning, Kerkula received his last dose of antibiotic injection, and pain medications before the nurse sent them on their way. He gave them another parcel of medications in addition to the one he had given them at the clinic. He walked them across town to the road, which led through the young forest, and said goodbye. He wished them good luck, turned around, and walked away. That was the last time Kerkula laid his eyes on the nurse, heard from him, or visited Botota. He made several attempts during his stay in Saye Wheh Town to revisit Botota but never did. The lack of available transportation and the difficulties one had to go through walking by foot were deterrents that made Kerkula and the others not to visit the town again.

THE CONFRONTATION

Soon after they had returned to the village from Botota, Kerkula was informed about what had happened in Saye Wheh Town early on the morning when he was carried to Botota for treatment. He learned that his soon-to-be mother-in-law had gone out to Deacon J and his family's yard and started to verbally attack them in the open and throughout the village, accusing them indirectly of being responsible for what happened to Kerkula. She spoke in Bassa about the incident so that most villagers would understand the gravity of the situation. Though she spoke in Bassa and indirectly, it was cleared that she was speaking to Deacon J and his household. Throughout her assault, neither Deacon J nor any family member came out to confront or inquire from the woman why she was pacing back and forth in their yard.

According to some villagers who witnessed the assault, Uncle J and his family decided to stay indoors to avoid any confrontation or escalation of the situation. Other villagers who witnessed the confrontation knew about the relationship between Deacon J and Mother M. They were aware of how both individuals knew each other well. It was said that both Mother M and Deacon J did not have a direct relationship, but there was an intermarriage within both families. Mother M had grown up around Deacon J's family and had known him when he was growing up. She also knew very well some of the traditional and cultural activities his family was involved with, and all that had happened to them over the years. She was cognizant that the family, especially Deacon J, had been accused several times in the past by some residents for being involved with the act of witchcraft. She had never stood up to the family before until the day it became clear that they were involved with the pain and suffering Kerkula had endured.

Even though Kerkula was not present to witness what had happened between Deacon J and Mother M, he wondered why she decided to put her character on the line and stood up against Deacon J and his family in the manner she did. He was fully aware she had become his mother-in-law, but it was not clear that she knew he had become her son-in-law. He had not been officially introduced to her and had not received her approval for a relationship with her daughter before the confrontation.

Traditionally, parental approval is considered a form of guarantee or ritual that must be received for a successful relationship or marriage to occur between two individuals, especially young people. However, there are times when nontraditional citizens may choose not to adhere to such rituals or formalities in getting married. Some may choose to ignore these rituals and get married regardless of the consequences.

In some African traditions as it is in Liberia, arranged marriages and relationships are considered appropriate and blessed when the parents of both individuals give their approvals or blessings before the marriage occurs. Parental approval or blessing is also considered an ancestral ritual which has been observed for decades in most West African countries, including Liberia. These are practices or traditional norms that have been instituted by our ancestors long before civilization.

Before the confrontation, Kerkula had not made any formal marriage proposal to Mother M's daughter because their relationship was young and on the brink of developing. However, he had contemplated talking with his host father, who shared kinship with Mother M and other members of the girl's family, to get to know them well. It was during the interim when the unfortunate incident occurred and changed his plan. He tried to circumvent the past incident and move forward with establishing peace and understanding between Deacon J and Mother M, but doing so successfully was beyond his control due to the existence of culture and traditional restrictions and ramifications. As you are already aware, Kerkula was not a member of any traditional societies or groups. His ability to engage those who were involved in these societies or groups was limited.

In some African as it is in Liberian villages, witchcraft activities are prevalent and can sometimes be viewed as a normal way of life. Saye Wheh Town was not one of such Liberian villages where witchcraft activities were common. Though real cases of such practices had been uncovered in the past, the town did not tolerate such practices, at least as the village elders had made it known. Unless a witch is caught in the act or there is physical evidence to prove otherwise that an individual is indeed involved in witchcraft activities, knowledge about him or her may not be a public cry but an accepted community phenomenon.

It is believed that there are several ways to confront a person who engages in witchcraft activities. In Liberia, witchcraft behaviors are handled by witchdoctors (aka medicine men). However, there are others whom I would like to refer to as "brave-minded" or "outlaws," like Mother M, who are willing to stand their ground and take matters into their hands based on personal convictions. These individuals are willing and prepared to deal with situations without permission from a council of elders or authority within the town. Usually, it is the ordinary people who are willing to risk everything to confront a witch. However, it is believed that these ordinary people are not ordinary in the first place. Some are traditionally or culturally connected or involved with other local groups and societies that promote or are against witchcraft activities at some levels.

While some residents of Saye Wheh Town widely assumed that Deacon J and his family were the primary cause of Kerkula's pain and suffering, there were no indictments brought on him or his family by the church, town chief, or elders. There has been no clear physical or legal evidence to suggest that Uncle J and his family were the primary reason for Kerkula's pain and suffering. However, based on cultural and traditional knowledge and practices, it is reasonable to believe that Uncle J and his family had some part to play in the pain and suffering Kerkula had endured.

We will never know exactly who was responsible for Kerkula's pain and suffering or why anyone in their right mind would decide to hurt a perfect stranger who knew nothing about their way of life and was not involved in any society or groups in the village that supported, tolerated, or conducted any acts of witchcraft activities other than being involved with church or religious activities. Also, we will never know why a "God-fearing man" would treasure evil in his heart for a fellow Christian.

Upon Kerkula's return from Botota to the village, he and J. Yarsiah went back to their room in Deacon J's house. They lived in it for approximately ten additional months before they were forced out of town by General "Mosquito" and his men. They lived in the house without fear and kept cordial relationships with Deacon J and his family like they did before the incident occurred. Though Kerkula was afraid at times, he had no option to seek accommodation elsewhere. Moreover, he trusted God to guide them throughout their stay in the village. He was convinced that since he kept no evil against Uncle J and his family and was not a part of any societal groups, God would protect them from all evil, known, or unknown. That remained his conviction until they left the town.

Ravi Zacharias said it right, "Evil starts without understanding purpose."[2] When we fail to seek the one who created us to understand why we were made but walk in denial of who we are, evil consumes us, and we lose our purpose. Interestingly, Deacon J lost his purpose and did not know who he was called to be. Matthew 6:24 reminds us, "No one can serve two masters. Either you will hate the one and love the other, or you will be

---

2. Zacharias, "Uncovering the New Spirituality."

devoted to the one and despise the other. You cannot serve both God and Money" (NIV). Equally, you cannot be a devoted Christian and a witch at the same time.

Even though an individual may have been physically involved with witchcraft activities, spiritually it is impossible for a Christian. Though we may claim to be devoted Christians and leaders of the church, the lives we live must represent the true meaning of Christianity. We should never allow those who can destroy our mortal bodies and not our souls to determine our purpose and how we should live our lives.

CHAPTER SEVEN

What Happens When Cultural and Traditional Practices Overrun Spirituality?

Spirituality is a deeply intuitive, but not always consciously expressed, sense of connectedness to the world in which we live.

—Richard M. Eckersley

There is a sense of relaxation in spirituality, but if spirituality is used as a seductive force, it could be the most destructive thing you have ever entered into because it gives you the feeling of being in contact with God when all you have ended up doing is defying yourself."[1] These are the words so brilliantly propounded by author and Christian apologist Ravi Zacharias when he answered the question, "Why do you think so many Christians in the West are looking to eastern beliefs for an answer?" Ravi's exposition of this question depicts a picture of what one may consider a true dramatization of the influence of culture and tradition in the church, especially the African church, and how they synchronize spirituality and Christian beliefs.

Elizabeth Lesser, cofounder and senior advisor of the Omega Institute, a holistic learning community in Upstate New York, defines spirituality as "a fearless investigation of reality" where one's deepest longings become a

1. Zacharias, "East and West."

compass for the journey. She listed ten dangers of spiritual pride, including narcissism, superficiality, instant transformation, grandiosity, ripping off religious traditions, the inner child tantrum, and the guru trip. "Spirituality is nothing more than a brave search for the truth about existence. Nothing more, but nothing less as well."[2] Additionally, two powerful cultural factors that work against spirituality in Western societies today are materialism and individualism, especially in combination.[3]

THE CHURCH IN SAYE WHEH TOWN

Before the advent of Christianity in Liberia, the country was strongly entrenched in African traditions, native religions, and secret societies. Most of these secret societies were characterized by spirituality and rituals.[4]

The church in Saye Wheh-Town was thought to be an icon of Christianity and a safe place for everyone, especially residents and villagers who, for the most part, disagreed or thought differently about the traditional and cultural practices of some groups or societies within and around the town. Some also regarded the church as the symbol of spirituality and a direct

2. Brussat and Brussat, Review of *The Seeker's Guide.*

3. Lesser, "Fearlessness"; Eckersley, "Culture, Spirituality, Religion and Health"; Zacharias, "East and West."

4. Gbote and Kgatla, "Role of Christianity."

contrast to secular and societal teachings and beliefs. However, culture and traditional beliefs held by villagers played significant roles in shaping their behaviors and depicted how they lived and interacted with each other and visitors.

> Cultures are about how we think the world "works": the language, knowledge, beliefs, assumptions and values that shape how we see the world and our place in it; give meaning to our experience; and are passed between individuals, groups and generations.[5]

Individuals who became members of the church in Saye Wheh Town separated themselves from some of the activities carried out by these groups that they considered contrary to their Christian beliefs. Consequently, the culturalists and traditionalists conceived a different notion about those who called themselves "Christians." They viewed the act of individuals calling themselves Christians as a contradiction to their traditional and cultural beliefs. The word "Christian" is also used by traditionalists and culturalists to refer to specific individuals who have successfully undergone traditional rituals, training, and graduation. They also believe that individuals who call themselves "Christians" use the word out of context or apply it wrongfully.

According to Focus on the Family, the term "Christian" "refers to anyone, man, woman, or child, who trusts in Jesus Christ as his or her Savior and Lord and who strives to follow Him in every area of life."[6] In Acts 11:26, it is recorded, "And when he had found him, he brought him to Antioch. And it came to pass, that a whole year they assembled themselves with the church, and taught much people. And the disciples were called Christians first in Antioch" (NIV). Also, the apostle Paul's letter to the Romans 10:13 tells us that "everyone who calls on the name of the Lord will be saved" (NIV).

Indeed, there is a misunderstanding or fundamental difference in definition of who is a "Christian" between the church in Saye Wheh Town and the traditionalists. As a result, the word "Christian" contextualized an ideological difference and hypersensitive reactions between leaders of the church and traditionalists. This issue remains a concern particularly for traditionalists today even as the knowledge of who is a Christian has become prevalent.

Before the arrival of Uncle Nat and his friends, the church's activities, which mainly consisted of Sunday worship services, Bible studies, evangelism, choir practices, and sport, were mostly done on Sunday mornings and

---

5. Eckersley, "Culture, Spirituality, Religion and Health."
4. "Definition of a Christian."

evenings because it was the common day off for most of the church members and nonmembers who attended Sunday worship services and other activities.

The arrival of Uncle Nat in the village and his willingness to assist with the church's day-to-day management brought relief to his oldest brother. He and Kerkula helped transform the ways spiritual matters were to be handled and conducted, which was in contrast to how it was done in the past. It helped boost new member recruitment, especially amongst the youth and first-time churchgoers, and structured the leadership of the church, including spiritual, administrative, and youth activities. The new management approach also helped to organize and plan lay readers' duties, preaching assignments, and evangelism.

The church soon began to take shape, and some villagers noticed the changes and momentum the new management approach had generated. The male chorus' activities and the traditional Bassa choir on moonlight sing inspiration nights helped galvanize more villagers to Sunday worship services.

It became clear, without a doubt, that the church in Saye Wheh Town had risen from its slumber and was now on the path to accomplishing the purpose for which it was established in the village. Membership began to increase steadily; the fellowship among the youth and adults became more cordial and harmonious. The youth and male chorus made conscious efforts to attend and support the traditional Bassa choir programs and vice versa. Christian values and a sense of spirituality that once seemed lost appeared to have returned gradually but more prominently. There were reasons to believe that the return of Christian values and spiritual mindedness to the church and village would last over a longer period and probably throughout the civil war because of the work Uncle Nat and his friends had already done.

It also became clear that young people were becoming fed up with violence and wanted to return to a life of normalcy. Their discontentment about the war was made known by their interactions, participation, and verbalization to church leaders, Uncle Nat, and Kerkula during youth gatherings and Bible study. Some of the youth wanted to disassociate themselves from the freedom fighter movement but could not easily do so for fear of their lives or of been labeled as renegades. Fortunately, the youth and church activities became a reasonable escape for those who had decided to abandon the movement and return to a life of normalcy.

The church began to play its role; a sense of togetherness and common respect for one another, which had disappeared due to the civil unrest, was felt across the village as though the wind of change had finally been unleashed. Engagements, Christian behaviors, mutual social interactions, and other guiding principles and activities became useful platforms by which the church increased the preaching of the good news.

According to Gbote and Kgatla, Christianity's role in the solidification of democratic processes within a nation is essential.[7] It helps to defend the fundamental rights of people against injustices and gross human rights abuses. Young people who became saved because of the Christian activities in the village looked to the church for solace and guidance. Some vowed not to return to the life of violence that they had once lived, while others failed in the process and returned to the movement. Those were the youth who later became problematic and a deterrent to other youth who wanted to become new members of the church or involved in its activities.

Despite the misconceptions held by some church members, some villagers were optimistic and hopeful about the new management approach and the direction in which the church was headed. They believed that the new changes were purposeful and would have lasted throughout the war and even when it ended. However, others became pessimistic and believed firmly that the new changes were just for a season. They believed the changes would not have lasted too long before villagers returned to their usual ways of life, and the church would have eventually lost its position once again.

Regardless of all the predictions and solemn beliefs held by villagers and other residents, Uncle Nat, Kerkula, and the others were certain that the new changes were good for the church's life and management. They believed the changes would have eventually produced successful outcomes contrary to the pessimism expressed by some church members. Kerkula, Uncle Nat, and his brother were convinced that they were in a good position to achieve better and lasting outcomes with the level of work they had put into developing the new management plans.

CULTURAL AND TRADITIONAL CHALLENGES

"When two different religious systems exist in one community, the tendencies of conflicts of socioreligious, ideological, physical, and even political characters will arise between them."[8] Equally, when the fundamental beliefs of two groups are contrary to each other, there will be challenges and difficulties in understanding and in the process of bridging the gap that exists between them.

It was apparent that the new direction in which the church was headed in Saye Wheh Town had been welcomed by many churchgoers and some

7. Gbote and Kgatla, "Role of Christianity."
6. Okeke et al., "Conflicts," 1.

members of the leadership team. Equally, there were many unexpected challenges that the framers of the new plan encountered along the way, which they had not anticipated. For example, during planned meetings at the church or the church's council, doctrinal or spiritual issues like baptism, tithing, leadership, and the balance between cultural, traditional practices and spirituality often took center stage and provoked arguments amongst the leaders. Once again, the use of the word "Christian" as it applies to those who are followers of Jesus Christ was often culturally misconstrued or interchangeably used to denote those who were members of the Poro Society. These were fundamental issues that the framers of the new management plan and all those who understood and supported it had to deal with daily.

Eckersley put it right when he said, "Cultural influences do not just change the external 'shape' of religion. Cultural messages can create tension, conflict, and confusion within individuals when they run counter to religious beliefs and teachings, making it harder to integrate religion into their lives. Culture can 'hollow out' the spiritual content of religion and fill it, instead, with other things, including materialism, nationalism, and fanaticism."[9]

The challenges facing the church in Saye Wheh Town were internal with its management and activities; it also had external consequences that impacted the village and prevented some non-Christians from becoming saved. For example, those who held leadership and spiritual positions in the church were also leaders of cultural and traditional societies. They fearlessly and unapologetically discharged their duties publicly as leaders and/or members of these societal groups. Some of these engagements made the church's works (e.g., evangelism, outreach, and preaching) more difficult and unfavorable amongst the same villagers whom they preached and witnessed to.

Another challenge the framers, especially Uncle Nat, faced was preaching in the church. Because he was a newcomer and leader of the church, he was not expected to preach or witness on any topics that would have underscored or outlined the contradictions of cultural and traditional practices held by some members and leaders of the church and that contravened the preaching of the gospel. He suffered verbal, supernatural, and often physical assaults for walking the other path toward preaching the gospel in its entirety and refusing to succumb to the ideologies and traditional practices of the leaders who opposed and threatened him.

Why are cultural and traditional practices that influence the church in Liberia, particularly Saye Wheh Town, important to this chapter's discussions? Simply put, currently, the church remains the only visible and authentic institution in Liberia that can bring clarity to biblical and spiritual

9. Eckersley, "Culture, Spirituality, Religion and Health."

understanding of Christianity and the role of culture and traditions, change moral, ethical conducts and the way of life of all Liberians, restore Liberia's relationship with Christ and encourage dignity in society, and restore Liberia's reputation and respect in Africa and around the world.

Though some may argue that the proliferation of religious denominations and organizations in Liberia affects the good image of the church, the difference is clear. The true church of Jesus will always be and has always been the beacon of hope where everyone, irrespective of their faith and religious beliefs, may seek refuge. Therefore, irrespective of the proliferation of churches, a need for the church to play its role in society at such a time in our history cannot and should not be ignored or taken for granted.

Due to the influence of traditional and cultural practices in the church at Saye Wheh Town, the following became setbacks to its spiritual and membership growths:

- *The church became stagnant spiritually but vibrant socially.*

Members who were not grounded in the faith and spiritual matters looked to find fulfillment and happiness in social, cultural, and traditional activities elsewhere and brought them into the church.

- *The separation and understanding of doctrine and dogma became a constant conflict and struggle amongst the leaders of the church.*

There was always a struggle between the pastors (Rev. G.G. and Uncle Nat) and the elders who held leadership positions within the church about what the Bible teaches and supports versus traditional and cultural teachings and values.

- *Power struggles and misrepresentation of leadership roles created pandemonium in the church's spiritual and administrative management.*

Church leaders who had positions in traditional and cultural societies wanted to exercise their authority within the church as they did elsewhere. They believed that their positions within the local societies should allow them the right and privilege to become leaders in the church because they saw the church and society as the same.

- *Church membership declined.*

Members, especially those who were new to the faith, eventually recognized the confusion of doctrine and dogma because of the influence of cultural and traditional practices and decided to discontinue their membership. Some went to different denominations, while others decided to abandon Christianity and return to their traditional and cultural societies.

The conflicts brought about by traditional and cultural practices influencing the church were not unique to Saye Wheh Town. Studies show that the influence of culture and tradition has impacted the church in Africa for decades and continues to this day. For example, religion in Igbo traditional society partakes fully of all the features of world traditional religion, including its beliefs, sacred myths, oral qualities, strong appeal to the hearts of adherents, high degree of ritualization, and possession of numerous participatory personages such as officiating elders, kings, priests, and diviners.

As the world moves deeper and deeper towards the commercialization of the gospel, there is a sense of urgency to reveal the truth about our past and current societies, communities, and cultural and traditional practices that have held many Liberians captive and led them into believing the corrupted evidence of supernaturalism and falsehood as though they were true. Liberians who continue to struggle with a balance between cultural and traditional practices and the acceptance of the good news of Jesus Christ must reckon with the truth of knowing that though the church exists and operates within society, no levels of influence from the society, an individual, or a group of people are worthy to supersede or undo the demand for spirituality within the church.

Matthew Parris, a confirmed atheist, once wrote, "In Africa, Christianity changes people's hearts. It brings a spiritual transformation; the rebirth is real, and the change is good." He went on to say, "Removing Christian evangelism from the African equation may leave the continent at the mercy of a malign fusion of Nike, the witch doctor, the mobile phone, and the machete."[10]

If the church is not preserved and kept sacred and independent of our cultural and traditional beliefs and practices, there would be no other institution left to guide us against society's ills and the wickedness of the Evil One. The church's presence and role in society will always guarantee our moral rectitude as a people and nation. At no time should cultural and traditional practices influence or supersede the spirituality of the church. Though the church exists and operates within society, it is the church that must influence and bring about changes and not society. The culture and traditional beliefs of humanity are not equivalent to or above the church's spirituality but subject to its teachings. Therefore, it is a dangerous precedent and a threat to the spiritual framework and growth of any nation when traditional and cultural practices prevail over the church's spirituality.

---

8. Parris, "I Truly Believe Africa Needs God."

CHAPTER EIGHT

Animal by Night, Human by Day—A Supernatural Encounter

The interaction between witchcraft and traditional healing, on the one hand, and the natural world on the other, is an interaction between the "supernatural" and the natural.

—Petrus and Bogopa

They say love makes you do crazy things, some as crazy as to make you act out of character or to endanger your life. I guess this was the same way love compelled the angelic hosts of heaven (angels of God) to act out of character when they saw the beautiful daughters of men, came down to the earth, and had offspring with them (Gen 6:1-4, NIV).

Unlike the angelic hosts, mortal man does not have the power to ascend into the heavens to seek romantic relationships with the angels of God; neither do they have the power to transform themselves into supernatural beings at one point and reincarnate at another, as some cultures, religions, and cult societies like the New religious movements (e.g., Theosophical Society, Eckankar, Scientology, Sai Baba, Osho, etc.) have established as a belief system. Reincarnation and supernatural power are intended for heavenly and angelic beings and not for mortal man.

Reincarnation, also termed as "rebirth," "metempsychosis," "transmigration," or "palingenesis," is derived from Latin and literally means "to take on flesh again." It simply means that we leave one life and go into another; it is all for the sole purpose of soul development and spiritual growth.[1] On the other hand, "supernatural" means something that cannot be explained by the laws of science. It is beyond science's approach and relates to a superstition that science cannot explain.[2] At least the Holy Bible does not give any indications or records of a time when God gave supernatural or reincarnational powers to humankind. Therefore, if a mortal man engages in such acts, it interferes with his spirituality and faculty and the faculties and spiritualities of those around him who are not involved or associated with such an act.

A LOVE STORY ENDS TRAGICALLY

This is a true story about a young man whose life was ended because of his involvement in a supernatural engagement or an act usually termed as "witchcraft."

It was early in the morning, and most of the villagers had already left for the gold mines and local farms. Few villagers were still in town. Some had taken the day off from work because it was the weekend, while others decided to sleep in and go to work later in the day after completing their morning routines.

The sun began to rise from the northern horizon, and local birds greeted the villagers with their melodious voices as though the symphony orchestra were performing. Their renditions of early morning squawking and chirping, usually done by other birds in different forests, were spectacular and entertaining. They captivated the attention of some villagers who were on their way to work.

Uncle Nat and Kerkula were up early that morning and sat in front of Uncle Nat's brother's house. As usual, Uncle Nat and his brother, Rev. G.G., woke up early each morning and sat before his house to catch the morning breeze, drink lemongrass tea with different spices, and talk about the church and family matters before Rev. G.G. left for his farm beyond the hills. This morning, his brother left the village early with his family. It was harvest time; birds and animals constantly visited and destroyed farms. Therefore, they had to be on the farm early to drive away the birds and animals that visited each day to eat rice and other fruits.

1. Nagaraj et al., "Mystery of Reincarnation," 83.
2. Efrizah, "Supernatural Power," 267.

As both men sat in front of the house and talked about their plans and watched the villagers moving back and forth, suddenly, a voice cried out, "Gboweh! Gboweh! Come and see, something is happening to this boy in your uncle's house." It was the voice of a middle-aged lady. She was the wife of Uncle Nat's cousin. She spoke in Bassa hysterically as though the earth were falling or the village under siege.

The sound of her voice alarmed the neighbors and bystanders that some began to run to the house where she directed them while others felt frightened and hid inside their houses and huts. Uncle Nat was still seated in his bamboo chair, resting against the wall with his feet up. He seemed not troubled or interested in what the woman had said. On the other hand, Kerkula seemed a little uneasy, concerned, and did not know what to do. "Sit down, Kerkula, and let's keep company! Don't listen to what the lady is talking about. They do this all the time to instill fear in others. She is probably having a moment," Uncle Nat told his friend.

It troubled Kerkula even more, to see that Uncle Nat paid the lady no mind and was not interested in verifying the information she gave them, especially knowing the period in which they were living. He thought it was almost out of character that his friend acted in such a way. But Kerkula did not know who this woman was or her relationship with his friend. During one of their nightly conversations, Uncle Nat had mentioned to his friend a struggle one of his cousins was experiencing with his wife. He told him that his cousin was struggling with deciding to divorce his wife because the traditional witch doctors had caught her participating in a ritual that involved members of a witch group from another village, which created a conflict that remained unresolved between the two groups. She was discredited, condemned, and excommunicated indefinitely, and stripped of all privileges. She was not taken seriously by anyone for anything she said or did whatsoever. Everyone but newcomers like Kerkula knew that about her.

His mindset toward the lady changed after his friend informed him about who she was and what she had done. However, he found the information which the lady gave them to be credible because of the number of people who ran to the site. He decided to go and verify the information personally. Remember, Kerkula was from a military family. He was always keen on verifying any information that could create pandemonium or security unrest. He was never complacent with unverified information or situations, especially amid a civil war. He became troubled when rumors of expected armed aggression on the village were not totally substantiated. Maybe it was the security-mindedness in which he emulated his father. Some of his friends always thought he was just too sensitive to crises or blatantly scared. He was neither moved nor troubled by his friends' opinions of him. He believed being complacent with unverified information during any crisis was a sign of mental weakness (lacking the ability or desire to think) or a portrayal of an "I don't care" attitude.

He told Uncle Nat he was taking a walk and would be right back in a few minutes. The moment he left his friend and turned the corner between the house and the kitchen, he came upon a gentleman he had never met before.

"Hello! You look strange. I have not seen you in town before. What is your name, and where are you from?" the gentleman asked!

In response, he said, "My name is Kerkula. I am a friend of Uncle Nat. We recently came to town—actually, on the day before yesterday."

"Do you speak Bassa?" the gentleman asked.

"No, I do not!" Kerkula responded.

"Well, my name is P.G., I live in this town in the house over there." He pointed to one of the nicer houses in the village.

It turned out that P.G. would become the bridge between Kerkula and his newly found relationship—a relationship that transcended the borders of Liberia, Guinea, Ivory Coast, and Ghana. As both men walked and talked, P.G. asked Kerkula, "Would you like to join me? I am going down to the house where everyone is headed."

"Sure, I would love to. In fact, I was headed in that same direction when I saw you," Kerkula replied.

Both men continued their walk together and reached the house where the incident had occurred. They were met upon arrival at the house with a graphic but supernatural scene, one Kerkula had never imagined or experienced before. It was a scene not common to everyday life but one that you could read about in a fictional book or see in a horror movie. It was dramatic and scary, at least in the eyes of the ordinary people like Kerkula who stood around. The scene would eventually challenge Kerkula's faith and leave him with many unanswered questions. It also forced him to reevaluate and reconsider his decision to either stay in the village or leave.

The entire backyard of the house was crowded with people. Some were gold miners who were on their way to work but had stopped by the house due to the noise and graphic scene that was unfolding, and others were farmers who had delayed going to their farms that morning. Some local merchants had come to town during the weekend to trade or purchase gold and were leaving for their respective destinations, while other villagers took the day off and stayed home. Interestingly, there were no kids around but a few females. There were a couple of older folks in traditional Liberian attires going in and out of the house and middle-aged men who spoke mostly in Bassa. No female could enter the house where the men who wore traditional clothing were meeting. The men seemed to have been in control of what was going on and understood exactly what had happened to the boy lying on a piece of traditional mat made from bamboo tree.

Kerkula overheard a bystander talking about what had happened to the boy lying on the bamboo mat and became interested. He became increasingly troubled by what he had seen even though he was looking from a distance. As he turned to talk with his new friend, P.G., and ask him some questions about what was going on, he realized that P.G. had left him standing alone by the side of a rice kitchen and moved closer to where the boy was lying. He caught up with him and asked, "What is going on here?" as he tapped P.G. on his right shoulder to get his attention.

"Umm," P.G. stuttered for a moment as he struggled to find the right answer to Kerkula's question. "I am not sure how to explain this to you, Kerkula!" P.G. replied. "You may not fully understand what you are looking at even if I explain it to you in the best way possible."

"It doesn't matter, just tell me. I would like to know," Kerkula muttered. He was careful not to let others know that he was interested in knowing what had happened because he was a stranger in town who was heavily engaged in the church's activities and not the culture and traditional practices of the villagers. Also, he was unsure if P.G. would have been willing to disclose the true story behind the boy on the bamboo mat.

As the conversation went on between the two men, P.G. turned around, looked his friend in the face, and asked him, "Are you a member?"

"A member, yes, I am a member!" Kerkula replied.

"What do you mean by a member?" P.G. asked.

"A member of what?" Kerkula asked. "I am a Christian if that's what you are asking about."

"No, I would like to know if you are a member of the Poro Society," P.G. stated.

"I have heard about the 'Poro Society,' but I am not a member and do not intend to be one," Kerkula responded sharply.

"No problem. I was not sure if you were or were not," P.G. responded. "I needed to know your membership status before giving you more information than you need. Come over here and let me tell you exactly what happened."

He took Kerkula for a short walk away from the crowd, put his right hand on his left shoulder and said, "It is said that when the crops reach full maturity and harvest time comes, the moon usually comes out at night and shines brightly in the clear sky. Young lovers and old alike are usually out merrymaking throughout the villages. It is a time when traditional and cultural festivals are held in the brightness of the moonlight. Villagers would gather around fireplaces and under palava huts and talk, drink, and eat throughout the night till dawn. Young girls would sing beautiful songs of love, heroism, togetherness, hard work, and family life at the top of their lungs, while others played the Calabash Shekere [aka "sasa"] and danced. Men would beat on Djembe and Conga drums made from animal skins, play the harmonica, traditional recorders made from local woods, and glockenspiels made from bamboo, and blow bull horns to entertain the others, especially the elders or village leaders. There would be plenty of sweet wine retrieved from bamboo or palm trees, fresh vegetables, bush meat, and a bundle of new rice gathered from the farm and brought to complement the night's festivities. It is usually a time to relax and celebrate the blessings which the gods of their ancestors (e.g., the gods of the harvest, sunshine, moonlight, rainfall, etc.) had bestowed upon them for a successful planting and harvest season."

He paused his narration for few minutes, walked few steps forward, turned around, and said to Kerkula, "Pay keen attention to what I am about to tell you; it might change your life forever. . . . This is also a time when some mortal men seek to supernaturally distance themselves from human existence and the gathering of their kinsmen to take on the forms of animals and enjoy supernatural festivities that are inconceivable and unnatural to the naked eyes."

In other words, these supernatural festivities are not visible to ordinary people, and only those who are members of such a gathering can attend. Those who know such supernatural activities believe that these events are mostly held during the night hours when the earth takes its rest or becomes silent. According to some villagers who are experts about these things, there are times when such events may occur during broad daylight, depending on the will or supernatural power of those involved.

In Romans 1:24–28 (NIV), the Bible tells us that humankind has become fascinated by God's creatures and not the creator himself. Verse 26 says, "For this reason, God gave them up to vile passions. For even their women exchanged the natural use for what is against nature." Also, in Romans 1:24–25, 28–29, the Bible tells us:

> *God also gave them up to uncleanness, in the lusts of their hearts, to dishonor their bodies among themselves, who exchanged the truth of God for the lie and worshiped and served the creature rather than the creator, who is blessed forever, Amen. . . . God gave them over to a debased mind, to do those things which are not fitting: being filled with all unrighteousness, sexual immorality, wickedness, covetousness, maliciousness; full of envy, murder, strife, deceit, evil-mindedness. (NIV)*

P.G. went on and said to Kerkula, "The boy lying on the mat under the kitchen recently relocated to this village from across the St. John River, where he once lived. Interestingly, during his stay across the river, he established a romantic relationship with a girl he loved dearly and was hoping to make her his wife. She was from a different tribe. Once upon a time, both tribes struggled to peacefully coexist through intermarriages even though they lived in the same district. It is believed that the young boy had gone across the St. John River to visit with his girlfriend one evening and was approached by two gentlemen, one of whom had declared his interest in the same girl the boy had gone to visit."

Before the young boy's visit and unbeknown to him, the same gentleman had gone to some members of the girl's family and expressed his intention to take her hand in marriage. Unfortunately, the girl showed no interest in him but in the young boy from across the river. It infuriated the gentleman and provoked him to confront the young boy. He told him never to return to the village to visit the girl and that he was not allowed to see her anymore. He spoke to the young boy as though he were the girl's parent or his father. The young boy paid him no mind because he knew that the girl loved and cared about him. He also knew traditionally that only the girl's parents or family had the authority to approve or reject his love for her. He ended his visit early that night and returned home safely.

A couple of months went by, and the young boy was invited by his so-called girlfriend to revisit her. This time, she had informed him that they would go out in the moonlight and play, but in a supernatural manner. This was a clear indication that both individuals belonged to a societal group or had something in common. It does not take much effort to explain or understand when members of the same group or those with common agendas speak the same lingo.

Apparently he understood his girlfriend's invitation very well and was excited to visit. Therefore, he planned his visit and awaited the day to come when he would travel by night to visit with his loved one. The night finally arrived, and he visited her. P.G. believed that the boy arrived sometime in the early part of the night, and both lovebirds went out to play in the moonlight as planned.

According to the story, they visited cassava patches and other farms around the village. They spent quality time loving on each other and celebrating the beauty of nature uninterrupted. By this time, both individuals had already been transformed from human beings to animals while enjoying their time together. Unfortunately, sometime after midnight and close to dawn, the young boy in his animal form fell into a trap and could not escape. He struggled, fought, and did all that he could do to escape the trap but failed. His unsuccessful attempts to release himself from the trap frightened his girlfriend, whom some villagers believed set him up to be murdered so that she would be free of him and could begin a new relationship with someone else. She decided to leave him trapped and escape to town since daylight was approaching quickly. She had to transform herself back into human form to avoid being noticed or killed by other villagers who might have gone on an early morning hunt for animals.

It is assumed in an African village that animals are usually found in farms around villages during the early morning hours. They come by night to eat crops in the local farms and are not mindful of the break of day or the rising of the morning sun. Therefore, farmers who leave town early during the morning hours to get to their farms are often lucky to encounter some of these animals and kill them.

Daylight was approaching quickly, and nothing the boy had done was enough to save his life. The girlfriend whom he had depended on was gone. He was left alone to fight for his life. "Animal by night and human by day," the young man struggled all night in both forms of existence to escape being trapped but failed. His body was brought outside in broad daylight from his room in human form and placed on a bamboo mat for others to see.

Kerkula became increasingly bemused as P.G. narrated the story of how this young boy became trapped supernaturally across the river, yet his physical human body was lying on a mat before them. He was more perplexed as he watched the young boy crying and fighting for his life like an animal about to be slaughtered or a frightened wildcat. He was convinced that the boy's misfortune was purely an act of witchcraft and nothing else. He had never in his life seen anything like that.

Once upon a time, Kerkula had heard his grandparents and neighbors he lived with talking about the act of witchcraft, but he had never come close to seeing one in progress. In fact, he was once told by his late uncle that his little sister, the only girl from both parents who died in 1980, was killed by a witch who lived in their neighborhood several years ago. He was never concerned or troubled by a witch or the idea of someone who claimed to have supernatural power and the ability to take another person's life until he came face to face with the boy on the mat.

Some people believe that witchcraft or the act of being a witch exists, while others do not. However, in a court of public opinion or looking through the lenses of critics, idealists, and even some of the villagers who stood around the scene, they could suggest many interpretations from different jurisdictions about the act of witchcraft in symbolic terms. A naturalist might see the act of witchcraft as somewhat normal or as an acceptable tradition and cultural way of life for a person or group of people. At the same time, a spiritualist believes it is a means by which humans interact with their dead relatives. A theist sees it as an abomination against the divine will of the Almighty God. Nevertheless, an existentialist may view it as the right and freedom of the individual to choose the life they want to live, whether natural or supernatural. Equally, a realist might consider witchcraft for what it is and deal with it without any pretense, while an atheist might view the act of witchcraft as being unique and having higher power than normal. A Utopian might consider witchcraft as a person living in an ideal or different world while maintaining a human likeness in the real world.

As P.G. concluded his narration of the boy's story, Kerkula was speechless and bewildered. He could not fathom how a human being could remain transformed and be in two places simultaneously, even though natural science suggests otherwise. He turned to his friend and asked, "Why did you decide to trust and tell me about the boy's story, knowing that I am not a member of any society or a member of this village?"

His friend chuckled and replied, "I told you all about his story because I have heard and seen what you and Gboweh [aka Uncle Nat] have done in this town to change the mindset of our people, especially the youth, within the few months you've been here. I believed narrating the boy's story would give you a better understanding of the dark world in which some of us grew up and are struggling to leave. This is the first incident you have witnessed, but it will not be the last that you will likely see in this village if you stay longer."

"Has there ever been a similar situation before?" Kerkula asked.

"Are you a member of any society?" He continued with questioning his friend.

"Why do you ask so many questions?" P.G. asked. "I don't have time to answer all of your questions, especially when this is going on before our eyes. There are too many conflicts of interest and traditional secrets that I cannot talk deeply about to you. I could have said more to you, traditionally if you were a member of the Poro Society, but you are not!" P.G. exclaimed.

"I totally understand; however, questions do not need an answer, but people do. That is why I am asking you all these questions," Kerkula replied. "I am curious to know these things because I would like to know. Moreover, I do not want to miss this opportunity since I have you here to tell me all about it."

Kerkula was taken aback even more so when his friend decided to tell him deeper insights into what the boy was going through and what it meant to be a part of such a cult society. He was reminded of and captivated by the words of the psalmist in Psalm 139:14, which says, "I praise you because I am fearfully and wonderfully made; your works are wonderful, I know that full well."

He turned to his friend and said, "We, referring to mankind, make a cardinal mistake when we misconstrue and incorrectly apply God's handiwork or 'blueprint' of 'fearfully and wonderfully' creating humanity in his image as giving man the power to super-spiritually or supernaturally do whatever he wants to do with his or her life. In man's infinite knowledge and deceitful heart, he has chosen to lower his standards and the authority God has given him above all creation to take position beneath or with the animals. Therefore, one may assume that man's creation will become his destroyer, and his rebellion against God will eventually create a platform for resistance against each other. Scripture reminds us in Romans 8:5–8, 'Those who live according to the flesh have their minds set on what the flesh desires, but those who live by the Spirit have their minds set on what the Spirit desires. The mind governed by the flesh is death, but the mind governed by the Spirit is life and peace. The mind governed by the flesh is hostile to God; it does not submit to God's law, nor can it do so. Those who are in the realm of the flesh cannot please God.'"

We will never know the true reason why the boy chose to become an animal by night and man by day. We will not fully understand what the boy went through lying on the mat in agony and losing his life in the presence of his fellow villagers unless we understand the cult he belonged to or the rationale of its members.

It was somewhat difficult to tell who was a member of the cult society by looking in the bystanders' eyes at the house where the boy lay. However, one could presumptively conclude that the elders wearing traditional attire who went in and out of the house where the boy lay knew exactly the nature and gravity of the incident. They also knew what the outcome of the incident was going to be even before the boy's demise. Unfortunately, no one other than the elders (aka, "Zoes") could understand or do anything to intervene in the boy's predicament but could only stand back and watch him fight for his life. His struggle to save his own life lingered for a long time while the elders discussed the way forward.

Hours went by, and nothing seemed to have changed. Villagers who stood by the house started mixed conversations about the boy's fate. Some predicted that the elders would have rescued him. However, there were others who seemed to have known more about the boy's situation and presumably had been somewhat connected and became more vociferous about the inevitability of his demise. The conversations became a little tense and loud enough that they attracted some elders who were standing outside. P.G. and

Kerkula remained nonparticipants in the conversations that were going on and returned to their initial position closer to the house.

As the sun began to rise and the conversations intensified, bystanders began to walk away. Time was passing by so quickly, and farmers who had stopped in their tracks to witness the young boy's entrapment were getting late for their farms. With more villagers gone, the surrounding areas became quiet, and soon, the boy lay alone on his dying bed. P.G. and Kerkula had to leave because everyone had left. It was the last scene of a mysterious death Kerkula had to come face to face with. To this day, Kerkula cannot figure out how can a mortal man became an animal by night and a human by day.

He still struggles occasionally with nightmares from the scene of the boy lying on the mat. It plays over and over in his mind every time he thinks about Saye Wheh Town. Even though he later learned from his friend that the boy had lost his life in the process, he will never forget the opportunity God gave him to witness the power of darkness and man's desire to live in a supernatural world where he has no controls. Some of the witnesses who were at the scene will never know why the young boy was engaged in such an act. They know that love can make a person do crazy things even to the peril of his or her life.

CHAPTER NINE

A Mysterious Birth

When human beings began to increase in number on the earth and daughters were born to them, the sons of God saw that the daughters of humans were beautiful, and they married any of them they chose.

—Genesis 6:1–2, NIV

There is an adage in Liberia that says, "A pregnant woman who walks the dark hilly paths at night is likely to give birth to a resident of the hills." This can also be interpreted as a pregnant woman who habitually travels back and forth on a farm road at night or when it is dark is likely to give birth to a child that may most likely take on an abnormal human identity. For this and many other reasons, husbands who farm beyond the hills or in deep forested areas away from a village would usually travel back to town during the early hours before sunset. This is done to avoid traveling back to the village late at night with their pregnant wife or wives. However, there are no known scientific theories or explanations to prove these assertions. Nevertheless, these assertions have become acceptable traditional beliefs amongst some traditional Liberians.

It is also said that the hills have eyes. In the same ways, some traditional Liberians believe the hills also have ears and can hear the faintest cries or talks, especially at night. Therefore, families who engage in farming in forest areas or hunt in the hillside would avoid talking at night or making noise while traveling in the dark. They believe at night, unusual creatures, animals, reptiles, and even those belonging to the demonic world will come out and move about the face of the earth. Making noise at night, especially in dark places, may put an individual or his family at the disposal of these creatures.

On the contrary, some also believe that making noise while walking in the dark may drive away harmful creatures. While the truth about these two beliefs is yet to be established, it is widely believed that being afraid of the dark areas or scaring off harmful creatures depends on the individual or family in the situation. Some individuals or families can relate to supernatural activities or fight back harmful creatures because of their connections or involvement with them. Therefore, they are not afraid of the dark or creatures living in it.

Once upon a time, M. Brown, the girl who came to Saye Wheh Town with Uncle Nat, Kerkula, and J. Yarshiah, gave birth to a mysterious baby. Before the child was born, her mother periodically went to assist on the farm beneath the hills. Their host, Rev. G.G., and his family were involved with local farming along the banks of the St. John River. Even though he was the local church's senior pastor, he cultivated the habit of self-sufficiency and engaged in large-scale self-sustainability initiatives like agriculture and animal farming to provide food for his family at such a time when the civil war had made life more difficult.

He planted a huge rice farm and local produce, including peppers, eggplants, garden eggs, cucumbers, butter beans, okra, etc. His farm's size demanded more human resources to protect it from animal invasions, maintain the crops from spoilage, and harvest when the time was right. Unfortunately, he did not have the workforce in his family to meet this demand until the arrival of his younger brother and his friends.

Uncle Nat and his friends' assistance to his brother's farming initiatives had tremendous impacts on the family's farming season. The family could harvest more produce and store more rice in the kitchens both on the farm and in the village, which sustained them throughout the rainy season. However, for Uncle Nat, there were some unexpected disappointments, and hardships that his friends, especially M. Brown, endured. She became pregnant several months after they arrived in the village. Her pregnancy was unexpected, and it changed her life forever.

THE BIRTH OF A MYSTERY BABY

What was expected to be good news of childbirth later became a public disgrace to M. Brown in the eyes of those who never knew or understood the meaning of giving birth to a mysterious baby. For some traditionalists, it was just another disappointing outcome of a pregnancy. They had already predicted the outcome of M. Brown's pregnancy long before the time of delivery. It was no surprise to some of the villagers, especially the elders who showed up at the house, when the baby's birth and the circumstances surrounding her were announced throughout the village.

Before she became pregnant, M. Brown was active, defensive, and a talkative individual. She did not hesitate to voice her opinions when it concerned her character or ideologies. She was passionate about the things she believed and spoke about them emotionally and emphatically. Other ladies at church and in the village knew this about her. Though she was a stranger in town, it did not bother her or deter her from confronting anyone who spoke negatively to or about her. She was a member of the Sande Society. She was sociable and had a moral rectitude and an upbeat spirit. M. Brown was hardworking and did not easily give up when helping with the farm's duties. She was the reason their host father decided to plant different crops and increase the size of his farm. She was always willing to go to the farm even if the weather was good or bad.

Work on the farm was done daily except on Sunday when most villagers stayed in town for church services and social gatherings. M.B. did not miss a day of going to the farm. One interesting thing about her was that she loved to eat, especially fufu. Like her host family, M.B. could eat fufu seven days a week and not complain or think about it being a poor diet choice. Maybe this was one reason she took pleasure in going to the farm every day even when she was tired or did not feel well.

Their host family also cultivated a large cassava patch where they harvested cassava to meet the demand for fufu, gari, and other food made with cassava for their children and visitors. After M.B. conceived and the pregnancy became visible, folks in the village, including Rev. G.G., cautioned her about traveling along the hilly paths in the dark, but she paid them no mind. As usual, she would argue with anyone who tried to give her advice about disrespecting the cultural and traditional norms of the village. She would often disengage from villagers who lived within her community for days if they tried to lecture her about being respectful to others. Whenever there was a confrontation, she would isolate herself and often travel to and from the farm alone or go along with other villagers who farmed nearby. She often seemed fearless but took lots of uncalculated risks, which often had unfavorable outcomes.

On the morning of August 14, 2013, M.B. went into labor. Contractions lasted for a while. It attracted more midwives in the village to come over at the house where she was to assist the first midwife who had been contacted by Uncle Nat to deliver the baby. The delivery process lasted for approximately fifty to fifty-five minutes before a bouncing baby girl was born.

At birth, she looked healthy but a little overweight. There was no device available to record the actual weight of the little baby. However, some of the midwives who helped with the delivery process assumed the baby was approximately ten to eleven pounds at birth. She had an abnormal rectangular head with short, thick, fat fingers. Her body mass index (BMI) was astronomical for a newborn. There was little hair on her head. His skin was covered with dark hair on some parts of her back but was smooth and light-skinned on her stomach area. Her toes were just as short as her fingers. Her eyes popped out of the sockets as though she was afraid or trying to scare someone else. Her anatomy was segmented with lots of curves.

She entered the earth with a peculiar but excruciating cry. She would cry for minutes, at least ten to fifteen minutes at one point, and stopped for approximately three to five minutes and resumed another set of cries for ten to fifteen minutes. This became a cycle of cries and continued throughout the days and nights after her birth. The only time she slowed down from crying was when she was being fed or was asleep in her mother's or Uncle Nat's arms. She ate regular food like everyone else because there were not many food options, especially for newborns.

The war was raging, and baby food supplies were limited or not found at all on the market. M.B. and their host family would make all sorts of baby food based on the advice of midwives and elders from the town. She would give the food along with breast milk to her little girl periodically. They tried different ideas to comfort the child so she did not have to cry throughout the day and night, but none of their ideas worked. Instead, it made her condition worse, and she cried even more than usual. Her condition seemed terrifying each time they tried to find ways to help her rest or sleep without crying.

The news about a crying baby girl born in the pastor's house spread quickly throughout the village as though the villagers did not see the baby's mom when she was pregnant or did not expect that she would have given birth one day. Concerned villagers and visitors packed the yard to visit and see the mystery baby.

There were different explanations for why such a baby was born in the village, especially to a stranger who had come to seek refuge amid a civil war. Some believed that the birth of the mystery child by a stranger was a sign of punishment on the mother. Others believed that it was her mother's blatant refusal to listen to the elders about walking the hills at night that caused the mystery child's birth. However, some also believed that the child's birth was God's way of chastising her mother for being arrogant and disrespectful to the villagers, especially other females and elders who had welcomed, accommodated, and shown love.

All the explanations and falsehoods about the mystery child's birth had a tremendous impact on her mother. They created such a sense of confusion and embarrassment for her that she hid indoors most of the time. She refused to go out to the farm and did not come out of the house except during the night hours. She limited her interactions with others except those who visited the house to see her and the baby.

For days, she wondered why such a mystery could happen to her. She tried to figure out what she had done wrong that resulted in such an unfortunate situation. She questioned God many times as though he were standing right before her. She cried night and day about what she was going through, but nothing she could do changed the situation. She had to face the reality of what had happened to her and care for the child even though she had hoped that the little girl was never born. Uncle Nat, Kerkula, and J. Yarsiah were confused about the entire situation but did not know what to make out of it. They, too, could not understand why such a life-changing situation could happen to M.B., especially in a strange town. All they could do was comfort and pray along with her for God's intervention into her situation.

It took a little over a week for the little girl to survive on the earth before she died. The news of her passing spread quickly throughout the village, just like the news about her birth. Those who knew exactly what her birth and death meant seemed not to be surprised or troubled by her demise. Others who were innocent like Kerkula paid their respect to the child's mother and the bereaved family.

Though the child had passed, M.B. found solace in knowing that she no longer had to deal with the situation. She regained the strength to live her life again amid the embarrassment and disgrace she endured initially. She remained grateful to her friends and all those who had stood with her throughout her darkest days. She learned from the situation not to take for granted the elders' advice or anyone who shows concern and empathy during a situation. She learned to respect other people's cultures and traditions, regardless of who they were or where they came from. She recognized that each culture and tradition was unique to its people, and no one should disrespect them.

In the months following the mystery child's death, M.B. gradually reestablished her relationships and engagements with other villagers. She asserted her role as a member of the church and a respectable individual. She quickly regained likability and trust from the same church members and villagers whom she had once disliked and refused to associate with.

The public humiliation and disgrace M.B. underwent made her more careful and respectful. She decided that she would no longer go on the farm alone or travel during the night hours. She also decided not to give birth to another child until she had returned to her hometown after the war. She had hoped to begin a new life in the village even though she was away from home. Before the birth of her daughter, she had planned to become a gold broker and travel to other African countries like others and sell gold and bring back new goods to sell. She admired gold brokers who came to town to buy and sell goods. She always thought they were smart and looked good. She envied them and wanted to become wealthy.

Unfortunately, the friendships she established with other villagers were not on good foundations. Therefore, she was forced to live a quiet and peaceful life after her daughter's death and up to the day when the village was besieged by General "Mosquito" and his men.

CHAPTER TEN

Black Sunday

No sound is more distressing than the plea of the homeless. The cry expresses the pain of hunger, thirst, and disease, and denotes the fear of death, insecurity, and repression. The cry is not pretense, but a reflection of grim reality.

—Jake C. Miller

It was a few minutes past 2:00 p.m. GMT on a beautiful and bright sunny afternoon. The breeze was blowing nicely as trees waved their branches, and birds flew high up in the clear, blue, open sky. From all indications, it looked like it was going to be a nice day. Some villagers who had slept in or taken the day off from work as was usually done on Sunday were headed to the gold mines to put in few hours of work, which they often call "the hustle" to raise few dollars for the social times in the evening. Churchgoers returned to their respective homes a little late in the afternoon because the worship service had lasted too long. It was almost usual that regular worship services lasted one to two hours when there were no fundraisers or baptismal programs included in the service.

Other young men who had also taken the day off from work were beginning to assemble on the soccer field next to the road that led to the gold mines. Occasionally, on some Sundays, young boys and girls, and elders who were soccer enthusiasts, would gather on the soccer field and practice or engage in competitions with teams from other villages and towns. This was one way by which the village embraced its diversity, social gatherings, and community engagements. The village authorities also utilized this time to entertain vendors and residents from other villages and towns who had come to do business, visit relatives, and/or witness the soccer match.

Before starting the soccer game, Kerkula, Uncle Nat, and the other two had gone home from church, had lunch, and had casual conversations in front of the pastor's house. Later, Kerkula and J. Yarsiah went up to their room to take a nap because there was still enough time before the soccer game started.

For the most part, the village seemed peaceful and exciting. Everyone seemed to have been going through with their normal activities. As usual, the practice was going fine with a few interruptions from a couple of vehicles with fighters in them that came through the village and left a few minutes thereafter. There was nothing suspicious or to be concerned about at the time. All seemed to have gone as planned. Expectations for social gatherings at night, including a night of gospel sing inspirations, began to rise as the soccer players prepared to take the field for practice. As usual, it was Sunday, and the town was lively and engaging. Some of the villagers who were headed to the soccer field were in festive moods.

FROM FESTIVITY TO CHAOS

The soccer teams were dressed in their colorful uniforms, and young men and women were seen in beautiful jeans, shorts, and T-shirts. Some elders remained in their church clothes and went to the game. It was difficult to tell there was a civil war going on when you looked at how beautiful everyone was dressed up and having fun. One would think that the war was completely over for a minute and life had returned to normal. Unfortunately, thinking in such a way would have been an infatuation.

The soccer field was dried with green pastures, and everyone seemed happy and socially compatible. No one would have thought that on such a beautiful Sunday all hell would break loose. Had anyone ventured to predict such a day in the village, he or she would have been either mocked or ridiculed by the villagers. Even though there was still a civil war going on, some residents of Saye Wheh Town and other gold mining towns engaged in more social activities and showed fewer concerns about the effects the war was having on other people and places in other parts of the country.

The village had completed a hardworking week and needed an evening of socialization and merrymaking. Villagers were not willing to be bothered by any news that would have aborted their time of pleasure. They had to prepare their minds and bodies for another long week of farming and gold mining. There could be no substitute for this social way of relaxing.

On Sundays, social engagements and merrymaking were becoming acceptable norms that the villagers, especially young people, and vendors looked forward to. For young people, Sunday activities allowed them to dress up in their new clothes and tennis shoes, which they sometimes paid lots of money or even gold to purchase for themselves. Their parents did not have to bother spending money on them. They knew how to work and earn money for themselves. In fact, on most occasions, the youth did the spending and not their parents.

Also, vendors from other towns and villages used the time to conduct more business transactions. This was an ideal time to sell to more villagers and visitors in a single day and at the same location. Vendors did not have to put in more work to reach their customers because they were found everywhere. Besides, the village was not a large community. One could walk around the entire village in less than an hour.

As the festivities went on and more villagers began to enjoy the afternoon of socialization and engagements, words of a planned attack by a known and supposedly fierce rebel commander, General "Mosquito," penetrated the town like a wildfire. This was unexpected news, and no one saw it coming. Some villagers doubted the news source, but it became increasingly evident that the unexpected was about to happen. It was just a matter of time before it occurred. Villagers and visitors like Kerkula, Uncle Nat, and others who had experienced attacks on a town or village before dared not to take the news for granted. They made sure to leave the soccer field immediately as the news began to spread. Other villagers and soccer enthusiasts who buried their emotions into the game ignored the news and stayed on the soccer field.

THE ARRIVAL OF GENERAL "MOSQUITO"

As the news of the expected attack quickly spread, the village began to disintegrate, and parents began to run around the town in search of their kids like a bear thrusts through a forest in search of her lost cub. Those on the soccer field began to leave, and some villagers were noticed leaving town and heading to their farms and other villages nearby. Gold miners who went to work early during the day returned home immediately because the news had already reached them.

Unlike past attacks, there was enough time for the villagers to prepare and leave town before the arrival of General "Mosquito." They had been informed that the attackers were coming to town from across the St. John River. The attackers would first need to find a way across the river and walk few miles before reaching the village. However, it was difficult to determine exactly what time, which direction, or how many men would attack the town. The fighters were good at their craft and meticulous in launching unexpected attacks. There was no need to stay around the village and try to figure out these things. It would have been a blatant catastrophe to make such a decision.

The fighters, especially General "Mosquito" and his men, were not individuals to contend with or take for granted. Based on the information received from other fighters in the village about the general, it was said that he was one of the finest but most aggressive fighters within the National Patriotic Front of Liberia (NPFL). He had zero tolerance for mistakes and nonsense and took his fighting seriously. According to some villagers directly connected with the movement, General "Mosquito's" loyalty to Mr. Charles Taylor, leader of the NPFL, his bravery, and his unwavering confidence to win the civil war against other warring factions earned him deep admiration from the leaders of the movement and his fellow comrades.

For the most part, some residents in Saye Wheh Town were known for braving the storms whenever they heard about fighters coming to town; General "Mosquito's" attack on the village was not one to brave but one to escape quickly before it occurred.

More villagers mustered the courage to hurriedly gather any belongings they could lay hands on and started walking away from town. As mentioned earlier, no one knew which direction the fighters would have come, but the villagers knew one thing for sure, and it was not to go toward the crossing point at the banks of the St. John River. They had assumed that the crossing point at the riverbanks was the only possible area closer to the town where the fighters would have easily crossed. Due to some of these uncertainties, the villagers went in different directions and different groups. Some of the groups were larger and some smaller. Those who decided to go on their farms or take to the bushes were fewer than those who walked the opened gravel roads to nearby villages like Dean's Town and Yolo's Town.

Uncle Nat and his friends were still indecisive about which direction to go. As you may already know, it had not been too long since they had escaped from similar attacks in Bong Mines and other cities and took refuge in Saye Wheh Town. The memories of past attacks were still fresh on their minds, which made them more frightened when the news of the attack on the village reached them. At this point, the village was the only place they knew and believed could have provided their basic needs and protection for any unforeseen dangers. Unfortunately, Saye Wheh Town had become another battleground and an uninhabitable domicile, especially for Uncle Nat and some town citizens.

They had to leave town as most villagers did. However, some villagers stayed behind and braved the storm. Kerkula and his friends had no idea which way to go or where they would have stayed. Most of the towns and villages controlled by the fighters were either isolated or already populated with displaced people. Most of them had some daily freedom fighters' involvement or activities going on. It was almost inescapable and unbelievable for a village or town to be without a rebel or have a visitation from a fighter or group of fighters within a day, week, or month.

One of the strategies of the warring factions was to recruit locally. In order words, whenever a warring faction captured a town, they conscripted the young, able-bodied men and women into their movements and trained them to look and act like them. Some of the young men who voluntarily or involuntarily joined them were either sent to other front lines or trained to maintain security within their respective towns or villages. This is one reason why a freedom fighter was practically found in every town and village, whether large or small. It did not matter the town's population or its size; the fighters made sure to either visit, take residence, or control it.

Confused about which direction to go and where to stay, Kerkula and his friends pondered the idea of going further into rebel-held territories by way of Ganta since conditions in those areas were assumed to be relatively under control. Later, they decided to go to Ganta and wait there for a couple of days before heading to Gbarnga or toward the Ivorian border depending on the situations in each location at the time. However, they were cognizant that going to Gbarnga, the capital city of Bong County, would have meant they would be at the seat of the rebel movement and the mercy of its leadership.

In December 1989, after Charles Taylor and the NPFL Movement entered Liberia and eventually seized Gbarnga, they captured other towns and cities nearby. Mr. Taylor, the NPFL, and later National Patriotic Reconstruction Assembly Government (NPRAG) took residence in Gbarnga and maintained the city as the seat of government and its operations until the holding of democratic elections on July 19, 1997, in which Mr. Taylor won the presidency.

It soon became clear to Uncle Nat and the others that Gbarnga was not the best or safest place to go even though the fighters and other sympathizers of the movement made it seemed that way. They soon learned that all strategic planning for future operations, logistical supplies, reinforcement, and other activities emanated from Gbarnga. Therefore, they decided not to go that way immediately but stay in Yolo's Town for the night until daylight, at which time they would have decided on a better option.

Like Bong Mines, they were hoping that the situation in Saye Wheh Town would have changed, and they would have been able to go back. Unfortunately, there was no way of knowing if the town was saved because no one had come their way from the village. Therefore, on the same afternoon, Kerkula and Uncle Nat decided to formulate a plan that would lead them safely deep into rebel-controlled territories without problems from any fighter or group of fighters. Fighters were often found along the roads in vehicles at high speed or on foot.

The plan they decided on was to group all the people following them as members of the church in Saye Wheh Town. Uncle Nat became the pastor and spokesman while Kerkula became the youth leader and general secretary, just like the positions they held in the church. All group members were asked to call Uncle Nat pastor, and not necessarily by his legal name. They were asked to straightly follow the instructions they were given or be forced to leave the group. No one could speak independent of the group's spokesman but only through him. This was to prevent unforeseen circumstances and unwanted investigations by the fighters. This way, the rebels could not scrutinize an individual or ask him or her any questions. All they had to do was speak with the spokesman of the group.

However, there were times when a fighter decided to speak directly with a member of the group due to suspicion or unusual behaviors like a person being afraid, intimidated, shaking too much, unsteady, crying, or talking uncontrollably. At such times, Uncle Nat would jump in immediately and try to redirect the talks to him and allow the member of the group to walk away.

Most times, the fighters did not bother large groups of people that stayed together. The assumption was that the boys and girls, though in large numbers, would not have been considered enemies. Instead, they were perceived to be Christians and belonged to the church. Though there were times when some members of the group left and went their separate ways, for the most part, they were obedient and stayed together throughout the journey.

Before they left Saye Wheh Town, Mother M came up to Kerkula and asked him to take her daughter along. She did not want her to stay alone in the village when all the other young people were leaving. She said to him, "This is my daughter; I am giving her to you so that she can be saved. Take care of her and take her with you wherever you go. She is yours now! I don't want her to stay here and be raped or killed by a fighter. Please do me this favor and take her with you."

Kerkula was astonished by Mother M's consideration of him to undertake such a noble task but, at the same time, deeply honored to see an elderly mother entrust him with the life of her daughter. He was also not too surprised because Mother M had already sensed a developing relationship between her daughter and him. Therefore, it was much easier for her to trust him. Also, she did not have many options to choose from about her daughter's safety. She either risked keeping her daughter in the village and facing the unexpected, or sending her away with him. She chose the latter.

Before the attack on the town, Kerkula and Mother M had not established an in-law relationship, nor were there more interactions between them. He had not been officially introduced to her as a son-in-law. Therefore, he was unsure why she had such trust and confidence in believing he would have protected her daughter from danger. As a matter of fact, he was concerned about the safety of his own life and where he would live freely without any harassment or intimidation from anyone. Nevertheless, he honored her request and agreed to take the girl along with them.

THE VILLAGE WHERE IT HAPPENED

They traveled several hours throughout the afternoon and the early part of the evening into Kokoyah and made a stop in a small village in Nimba County where they spent the night. The village was empty. Most of the villagers had already fled town to their farms. There were at least three older men and an older woman still in town. One of the older gentlemen and the older woman who happened to be husband and wife were seated by a pile of blazing firewood under a palava hut. The other older man was alone on the porch of a mud building not far from the palava hut. It was apparent they were having conversations among themselves when Uncle Nat and those traveling along arrived in the town. At first, they thought Uncle Nat and the group were rebels. They tried to run away but soon realized these were displaced people seeking refuge. So, they welcomed him and his so-called church group and invited them to rest for some days in the town before continuing their journey.

The folks in the little town were hospitable and welcoming to Uncle Nat and his group. They provided them food to cook and eat, water to drink and take baths, and accommodations for the night. After talking with the elders upon arrival, Uncle Nat and some group members gathered around the blazing firewood under the palava hut and started keeping company. They sang gospel songs and danced while others who were not filled by the food they had eaten went to find additional food. Kerkula and a few others went into one of the buildings to make lodging arrangements since it was getting late.

They spent the night peacefully but remained on the alert for any disruptions. The next morning, most of the group members were up early while some were indoors and ready to continue their journey. Kerkula and Uncle Nat decided that the group would prepare and eat the food given to them by their stranger fathers before getting back on the roads. They cooked, ate, and rested a little before their walk started.

While resting and waiting for the time to depart, a couple of heavily armed fighters entered the town and sent shock waves throughout the village. Some of the group members under the palava hut fled to the northern part of the town into the nearby bushes and banana orchards, while others hid in the houses.

As usual, he did not flinch or run away. Uncle Nat remained standing and conducted devotion with the group members who did not run but sat in their respective seats even as the heavily armed fighters approached them. As for Kerkula, he had gone into the house to pick up a notepad and a pen upon his friend's request. Both men wanted to list all members of the group who had decided to go with them to Ganta. This was meant for accountability purposes and to prevent others who had the potential of causing chaos from joining the group. They took the necessary steps to forestall anyone from causing trouble, especially during their journey, which was critical to such a large group's cohesiveness and survival.

To their utmost surprise, the fighters had surrounded the entire village except for the road, which led through the banana orchards down to the creekside. A couple of fighters walked up to Uncle Nat and those under the palava hut and started interrogating them. Some went into the house where Kerkula and others were and forced them outside, while the rest of them stayed with their commander in the town square to monitor everyone's movement.

After several minutes of interrogations, the commander ordered his men to bring Uncle Nat to him. Before they reached the commander, a fighter in the house where Kerkula was began to loot. He took the backpack, which contained tennis shoes, belts, and some clothes, and walked away with it. The backpack belonged to Kerkula; he had brought it with him from Saye Wheh Town. The bag and everything in it were all Kerkula had and depended on throughout the war. It was the only bag that he took from Saye Wheh Town during the attack by General "Mosquito."

While standing at the back door of the house where he had been forced to conceal his identity, Kerkula spotted the fighter with his bag and walked quickly to appeal to him to give it back. Suddenly, the fighter turned around when he heard footsteps coming closer behind him. He asked, "Why are you following behind me, and what do you want?"

"Sir, the bag in your hand is mine, and I would like to appeal to you for it," Kerkula replied.

"What did you say? Who says the bag is yours and who gave it to you?" the fighter asked angrily.

"I brought it with me from Saye Wheh Town, sir," Kerkula replied.

"Sir and Saye Wheh Town? Are you a soldier or a gold miner? Is this why you are so brave to come behind me and ask for a bag?" the fighter asked. He continued, "You must be stupid to come after me asking for a bag. You must not respect yourself or value your life. Stupid boy!"

By this time, the fighter had become extremely agitated even as his colleagues tried to calm him down. He ordered Kerkula to walk before him and began to push him from the back. "I will teach you a lesson, stupid boy! You are a government soldier who has come on reconnaissance," the fighter said angrily.

He became vociferous and was not willing to listen to anyone. He pushed Kerkula from behind the second time with the bottom of his raffle. The third time, he stabbed him on his back with the bayonet, which was mounted on the muzzle of his raffle.

Upon reaching the commander seated on a wooden bench with fighters standing around him, he ordered Kerkula to lay flat on the ground with his face in the sand. The fighters standing around the area had all sorts of weapons in their hands, strapped to their chests, and on their backs. Some of them were dressed up fearfully beyond recognition, while the commander looked calm but alert.

"Who are you, and what is your name?" the commander asked.

"My name is Kerkula, sir," he replied.

"Why are you in this town, and where are you going?"

"Sir, we are a church group headed to Ganta," Kerkula replied.

"Why are you going to Ganta, and where did you come from?"

"We are going to Ganta to stay or go on to Gbarnga. We came from Saye Wheh Town," Kerkula responded.

"Is that the gold mines in Kokoyah?" the commander asked.

"Yes, sir!" one of his commandos responded before Kerkula could speak.

Before the commander could continue with his interrogation of Kerkula, the fighter who had stabbed him in his back stepped up and asked the commander to speak with him. "Sir, may I speak with you, please?" the fighter requested.

"Go ahead, soldier," the commander replied.

"This man, pointing to Kerkula laying on the ground, is a soldier of the Armed Forces of Liberia (AFL) and is on reconnaissance," the fighter insisted. "I arrested him in that house"—pointing to the house where he had pushed Kerkula—"because he was talking nonsense to me. Sir, I would like for us to make an example of this guy so that others will know that we are serious."

"What would you suggest?" the commander asked.

"Let's get rid of him as quickly as possible," the fighter replied.

The commander seemed troubled by the suggestion of his comrade. He looked younger than most of the other fighters who were with him. He was articulate and seemed to understand how to manage his men and address their requests. However, he seemed troubled with the request of his subordinate. "I don't think this boy is a bad person; neither is he a soldier," the commander said. "I think he is what he said he is, and I would like to believe him based on the number of questions I have asked him and the answers he has provided."

At that moment, it became clear that the commander had used his judgment not to execute Kerkula but to convince his soldier, who became frustrated and angrier because the commander had refused to consider and enforce his suggestion. Recognizing the frustration of his soldier, the commander decided to appease him openly. He called out to the church group members, "Who knows this man? If anyone knows him, he or she must come up front now or else, I will make my soldier to 'finish his business,' meaning execute him," the commander said loudly.

No one spoke a word or did anything. Everyone seemed to have been terrified, including Kerkula's supposedly girlfriend. She, too, said and did nothing as he continued to lie prostrate with his face still in the sand.

Once again, Kerkula felt abandoned by his friends and so-called girlfriend, just like he had felt with his brothers when he was detained at the Kakata police station on their journey to Bong Mines. He also felt a renewed sense of déjà vu and did not know exactly what was about to happen to him. Uncle Nat attempted twice to directly intervene by approaching the commander as the concern for his friend's life overwhelmed him, but an older man within the group quickly pulled him back. They suggested that Kerkula's so-called girlfriend would be the best person to speak up on his behalf and possibly set him free. Therefore, Uncle Nat went into the house where the girl was and encouraged her to go outside and speak on his behalf, but she refused. She claimed she was afraid for her life and did not want to be mistreated by the fighters.

It took a while, and no one spoke out or came forward from the group to rescue Kerkula. It terrified him even more, knowing that no one was willing to step up and rescue him. Amid his perplexity, he was sure of one thing, which was knowing that Uncle Nat would have done anything and everything to save him. He was convinced something must have gone wrong or been beyond his control, which may have prevented or delayed his friend from confronting the commander or his men. He knew it was just a matter of time before he would have done something to rescue him.

These two men had a good friendship. They trusted each other and would do anything possible to protect one another. Though Uncle Nat was older than Kerkula, he listened to him and respected his opinion. However, Kerkula had higher admiration for Uncle Nat. He considered him a mentor of the faith. He respected him for who he was, his knowledge of leadership and service to others, biblical principles, and survivorship, especially in times of crisis. Apart from the grace of God, Uncle Nat was one person you could trust and depend on for advice or help when you could not find a way out of a situation. He was a good human being.

Unfortunately, time was passing by quickly, and nothing had been done to engage the commander and secure Kerkula's release. Fortunately, God stepped in and performed yet another miracle in the sunshine. The commander began to focus his attention more on the direction where Kerkula lay. For some reason, he seemed concerned and wanted to take another course of action but was mindful not to appear weak before his men by allowing Kerkula to walk away freely.

Even though it had not been established beyond a reasonable doubt that the allegations leveled against Kerkula were true, the commander was hesitant to decide against his fighter's spoken will. Doing so would have made him look weak in the eyes of his men. He was fully aware that weakness was not an acceptable position within the movement, especially when you are the commander.

Based on other fighters' conversations, an instant replacement of a commander who exhibited visible weakness was inevitable and most likely instantaneous. They believed there was no reason or place in the movement for a fighter, whether a commander or subordinate, to fear anyone or decide to take any action that did not support his men's wishes or the movement. They also believed bravery and loyalty to the movement were true reflections and commitments to the values and ideals they stood for, fought for, and committed their lives to defend.

From all indications, the commander appeared to have struggled with indecision. However, time was not on his side. He had to decide quickly because the evening was approaching, and they had to continue their patrol to another village. As he gobbled down his dried rice with pepper soup and goat meat, he ordered one of his men next to him to bring Kerkula before him. He also ordered the soldier to bring a whip made from car tires. Apparently, they carried it with them from place to place torturing their victims, especially those suspected or found guilty without any court proceedings or legal defense.

"Sit down over here and look at me," the commander ordered Kerkula. "You looked like a good person. I want to believe who you said you are, but I am going to teach you a lesson so you will never do this again," the commander said harshly. "Lay down over here, and the soldier will give you twenty-five lashes on your butt for delaying our time."

Notice, the commander ordered Kerkula to be whipped not for the allegation leveled against him by the other fighter but for "delaying their time." This was the compromise he could easily reach to appease or placate his fighter and, in the process, save Kerkula's life. You could tell that the commander was not pleased with his soldiers torturing this innocent man, but he had no choice but to please them. One could argue that at some point in the commander's decision-making process, he may have become afraid for his own life. He might have been afraid that had he not appeased his soldiers, he could have been assaulted or harmed by any one of them during their patrol or in the line of fire. Unlike some of the commanders in higher authority, this commander seemed to be a farsighted young man who spent time contemplating his decisions before he made them.

After he made the decision to whip Kerkula, one of the soldiers on the commander's right-hand side reached down in his bag, pulled out a sizable piece of a cut-out car tire, and began to wiggle it in his hands. Kerkula remained in the same position and speechless. He did not know what he had done to deserve a beating, but he was thankful to God and the commander for saving his life from the hands of the fighter who desired so mercilessly to end it.

The soldier went back and forth, scourging him repeatedly on his butt and back. He remained motionless and defenseless throughout the humiliation as though his body were a punching bag or canvas. In the end, the commander ordered him to get up, shook his hand, and told him, "Be a good man and do not get in trouble again." Kerkula looked the commander in the eyes, thanked him, and walked away with blood running down his back from the wound caused by the soldier who stabbed him. He felt humiliated, disadvantaged, but thankful to God for giving him another chance to live.

He reunited with the others and his friend, who told him what had happened in his absence. They had watched him being mistreated by the fighters, but there was nothing they could do to rescue him. Uncle Nat disclosed to him the decisions they had made and his attempts to rescue him.

He thanked his friend and assured him that he knew that he would have stepped up for him if no one did.

They quickly regrouped and discussed their plan to leave the village after the fighters left. Before the fighters could leave the village, they seized a couple of young men who initially fled the village but returned by night because they were under the impression that the fighters had already left. They ordered the young men to carry their food and boxes of ammunitions to the next village. Due to the absence of the boys who were forced to go with the fighters, the group decided to spend one more night in the village to await them before leaving the next day.

The next morning, they woke up early to find out that the young boys had not returned. Therefore, they decided to leave town as conditions for food, health, and security deteriorated and became a concern for the group's leaders. They needed to leave quickly and get to a bigger and more secure place where they could be freed to move around and find food without harassments, intimidations, or fear for their lives.

EIGHT NIGHTS AND EIGHT DAYS

They entered Ganta early during the afternoon after walking several hours on the roads. Upon arrival in the city, there were movements of people back and forth. The city seemed relatively peaceful but heavily populated with fighters. Some civilians who were found in the streets were headed toward Gbarnga and Kakata with the hope of branching out to Bong Mines and other towns along the way, while others went toward Sanniquelle, Tappita, and the bordering town of Loguatou with the hope of either crossing over into the Ivory Coast or staying in towns and villages within the county. Also, there were others who came to the streets simply to find food and household products to buy for their families.

Though life in Ganta was somewhat peaceful, goods and services were in limited supply. The increase in population within and around the city subjected many residents and displaced people to hardship and rampant thefts. Some young people claimed to be freedom fighters but were not. They were street mongers and kleptomaniacs who engaged in looting the community and stealing from the residents. Some were apprehended and disciplined publicly by those in authority, while others were let go without reprimands. Finding food in the streets meant either one of the three situations: risking one's life, paying high costs, or being unable to find any food to buy.

Initially, they had planned on staying in Ganta for six days and six nights, hoping to receive good news from Saye Wheh Town so they could return and continue where they had left off, but the news never came. They had hoped for some ceasefire agreement among the warring factions, which would have enabled peaceful civilians to return to their respective cities, towns, and villages. Unfortunately, that hope seemed too farfetched and an evidence of a utopia.

Instead of the good news they had anticipated, words on the streets informed them that the NPFL was preparing for major consolidated attacks on Monrovia, Liberia's capital city, and other important institutions within and around the city. This was not the news Uncle Nat and his friends were hoping to receive. For them, ending the war and allowing Liberians to live once again as brothers and sisters in a country they called home was paramount over repeated offensive and defensive military attacks against each other.

The men were frustrated that the good works they had started in Saye Wheh Town with the youth and church, which had started to achieve momentum, were on the brink of collapse or had already collapsed. They recognized that the chances of returning to the town and continuing the works after the war had come to an end would have been more challenging or almost impossible. They had longed for a day when the impacts of their work in Saye Wheh Town would have transcended to other towns and villages and positively impacted the young people in those areas. Unfortunately, their longing for such a day to come was fading away without any hope for the future as the village's work had been abruptly sabotaged.

Days went by, and civilians' activities like selling, buying, looking for food, and visiting family members in the streets of Ganta began to vanish rapidly as the influx of militarized vehicles mounted with heavy artilleries and fighting men became visible daily. Based on observations, the evidence suggested that indeed well-coordinated and planned attacks were imminent, and an outbreak of another wave of hostilities against other warring factions was inevitable. Battle cries like "San-ga-lay-go-wa" and traditional war songs were sung throughout the day by fighters in the streets and those in vehicles preparing for the front lines. The frontline fighting battalion scene looked like a mighty army getting ready for war against another. According to Durkheim,[1] conflict is imminent in a society that is not held together by positive solidarity but by force rooted in greed, selfishness, and egocentrism.

---

1. Wood and Wood, *George Elton Mayo*, 93–98.

The thought of ordinary Liberians carrying deadly weapons in their hands, on their backs, strapped to their chests, and mounted on cars as they prepared to fight mercilessly against their brothers and sisters over issues that could have been resolved otherwise by seeking other workable solutions troubled Kerkula as he stood on a street corner and watched the fighters assemble for battle. It proved to him that indeed wars were masterminded by the elites in society, but it was the ordinary and vulnerable citizens, especially the youth, who must make the uttermost sacrifice with their lives during and after the war.

Brian J. Trautman once said, "War is the most act of terrorism and among the greatest causes of human suffering and death and ecological degradation. Wars are declared by the rich and fought by the poor. There will be no real justice and protection of human rights and the rights of nature until a sustainable peace has been achieved."[2] Liberians fighting against Liberians was not and will never be the answer to achieving lasting peace. Finding workable solutions to our disagreements and ideals through peaceful dialogues and engagements influenced by our desire to coexist peacefully is one of the best ways to resolve our differences instead of warfare.

Kerkula returned to the house where they were living with a heavy heart and frustration. Scared and discontented, he called his friend, Uncle Nat, and asked that he go with him to the room where he slept. Both men stood against the wall in his bedroom to talk because there was no chair or bed but a bamboo mat on the floor, which he slept on. He said to his friend, "We must leave town tomorrow or sooner. It is no longer safe in this place. I have seen a lot before, but what I saw today in the streets is enough to tell me that there are imminent dangers, and we need to leave town early before it gets too late."

"Where do you think we should go?" Uncle Nat asked.

"What do you think?" Kerkula replied.

"Maybe we should head back to Saye Wheh Town. Maybe, things are fine now," Uncle Nat suggested.

"Not a good idea!" Kerkula replied quickly. "You know we've been through this before; returning to a city which has suffered immediate attacks is not a prudent thing to do." Kerkula lamented, "I suggest that we take a leap of faith and leave the country for now. We can go away for some time and return home when conditions become favorable."

"Where do you suggest we go, and how do we do that?" Uncle Nat asked.

"My thought is, we should go into Guinea since the border is not too far from here. Going to the Ivory Coast like others are doing may be a long

---

2. Brian J. Trautman, quoted in Anderson, *Journey to Bong Mines*, vi.

distance for us," Kerkula whispered, since he did not want anyone in the house to hear him.

"Guinea! Why would you even think about going there?" Uncle Nat asked. "Do you know how to speak French or Mandingo? I don't!"

At this point, the conversation between the two men was becoming a little heated and uncomfortable because they could not reach a quick compromise. Uncle Nat seemed frustrated with the impossibility of returning to Saye Wheh Town. He wanted so desperately to go back and continue his work in the village. Therefore, he allowed his frustration to interfere with his decision about going to another city or country.

Realizing that his friend was becoming frustrated and upset with the entire situation, Kerkula asked that they pray about it, sleep on the idea, and resume talks sometime the next day. Uncle Nat agreed, and both men walked out and went to find food for everyone to eat. They kept the plan a secret from the others so that there could be no undermining or exposure. Sometimes it is good to keep some things a secret to yourself and not let everyone into it, especially amid a civil crisis.

The next day, the atmosphere outside was friendly, and the sun was shining bright. Both men met under a mango tree, which stood in the backyard, instead of going to the bedroom to continue with their discussion from the previous day.

"I have given our conversation from yesterday some thought and would like to share with you what I think would be best for us," Uncle Nat said.

"It is good you did. I also did, likewise. So, what have you considered?" Kerkula asked.

"I would like to believe you have given the idea of leaving Liberia and traveling to Guinea at this time a prayerful thought and consideration before suggesting it to me, right?" Uncle Nat asked.

"Yes, I did!" Kerkula quickly replied.

"I prayed about your suggestion last night before going to bed. I am convinced this is the best thing to do at this time to be saved and free from this chaos," Uncle Nat lamented.

"Thank God! I am glad we can agree on the same idea," Kerkula responded. Let us plan on leaving town as soon as possible before conditions deteriorate."

"Good idea!" Uncle Nat replied.

"Let us make sure that J. Yarsiah, M. Brown, and your friend are aware and support our plan," Uncle Nat cautioned his friend.

"Sure! Let's talk with them tonight about the plan when it is time for bed," Kerkula suggested.

"Ok, we will do that!" Uncle Nat replied.

Both men ended their conversation and walked away from each other. Kerkula returned to the main streets while Uncle Nat went in the house to find food to eat. Reminded by what his father had taught him about being prepared for war in times of peace, it was important for Kerkula to make sure that he knew his surroundings and exactly what was happening in his neighborhood. Therefore, he visited the streets each day to gather information, since he and his friends had no other newsgathering source.

He went to the main streets where the action was to observe the movements of civilians and fighters. By doing so, he observed and gathered current information about what was going on in the streets. He did not want him and his friends to be caught up in any situation that would endanger their lives. Therefore, he remained vigilant on daily newsgathering throughout the war even though there were times when he put his life at risk trying to understand what was going on in and around the various communities.

During the civil crisis, word of mouth or physical observations (seeing and verifying information for oneself) were two common ways by which information was gathered or received. However, some individuals, homes, and communities had access to electricity and electronic devices like radios, landline telephones, and television networks, allowing them to receive information daily even as the war was ongoing. Some of these were individuals, homes, or communities, like Bong Mines, LIMCO Yekepa, Buchanan, and Monrovia, that were considered privileged up to the time the war finally reached their communities because they had some levels of normalcy amid the raging civil war. Make no mistake, some of these individuals and households that enjoyed these benefits were protected by those in authority or associated with different movements. Therefore, they were able to continuously enjoy the fruits of normalcy until all hell broke loose.

THE EXIT

They stayed in Ganta for an additional two more days after spending six days and nights. Kerkula wanted to be certain that everyone had been informed and was on board with the plan. They had to make sure that going into Guinea as refugees for the first time was a safe and prudent idea to pursue. They also had to figure out how to leave town so that their departure was not noticed by those in the house or the fighters who lived in the same neighborhood. If someone noticed their departure from Ganta or uncovered the plan, it could be disastrous and might force them to abort their travel. They did not want that to happen to them. They had all intentions to leave Ganta and begin a new life on foreign soil for the first time. No obstacle or threat was prodigious enough to overturn their plan or change their minds from leaving Ganta. Therefore, their plan remained concealed, and the strategy worked.

They left Ganta one day before the launching of the attacks on Monrovia and its environs. It was the last time during the civil crisis that these five individuals went back to Liberia. They were forced to leave their country and settle in exile not because they wanted to, but because life at home had become more chaotic, difficult, and unpredictable. They had no choice or reason for staying in Liberia but chose to seek life and safety elsewhere. It was either stay in Liberia and go through the struggles and uncertainties or seek refuge somewhere else. Fortunately for them, Guinea became a good and timely opportunity.

They woke up early on the morning of their departure and started their final journey out of the country. The five individuals made sure to walk separately but in close distance to avoid any suspicions or concerns from anyone, especially a fighter. They did all they could do to avoid any delays to their trip. Had they encountered a delay like an arrest of one of them, it could have denied all of them the opportunity of leaving the country and landed some or all of them in jail based on the charges brought upon them.

Before the morning of the trip, Kerkula decided to locate the roads they needed to take to cross the border safely. He also inquired about the security checkpoints, the security guards' interactions, and what was needed to enable a person to cross the border without any problems. He shared the information with his friends, and everyone was fully prepared for what to do individually or collectively in the event that a fighter held back one of them.

They kept eyes on each other as they walked the gravel roads toward the border. Each one made sure to keep pace with the others so that no one was left behind. They also planned that everyone would slow the pace and wait if one were held back by a fighter or someone else. The others were not going to cross the border if one of them was held back for whatever reason. They managed to reach the border with no one left behind and without any suspicions or intimidations from anyone.

THE CLOSURE

Hopefully, what you have read in this book has challenged your imaginations and provoked you to become better Liberians and contributors to our society's development. Maybe this book has in no way changed your perspectives about what Liberia is or what it needs to be to regain its position and respect within the community of African nations. Whichever position you have taken or decision you have made about Liberia or your contribution to its development, let me encourage you in the words of Bob Marley. "Zion Train" is a song performed by Bob Marley and the Wailers. The lyrics of the song, which Marley wrote shortly before he died of cancer in 1981, center heavily on Marley's Rastafarian beliefs. The song's lyrics mainly see the narrator (Bob Marley) advising people to board the "Zion train," which according to him is coming their way. In his eyes, boarding this train will save their souls in the end.[3] Though his reference to "Zion Train" was meant to metaphorically paint a picture of a path or means of reaching a place, paradise, or heaven where we as a people must seek to travel, Marley also cautioned us to be wise and not gain the world and lose our souls, which is also recorded in the Holy Bible in Mark 8:36. Therefore, it is fair to say that the "Zion Train" that we must travel on as a people and country has already arrived and is about to leave the station carrying those willing and prepared to face the challenges of social and societal change in Liberia. He also cautioned us not to forget about our history but to know our destiny, because in the abundance of water, the fool is thirsty.

We must be mindful about the paths we have walked in our history so we do not return to them. With the abundance of resources that we have, we must look to ourselves, and not others, to make maximum use of them and develop who we are as a people and a country. Others will take our resources away from us if we are not willing and prepared to use them to develop a future for the next generations of Liberians.

Fifteen years of civil war has come and gone, but the memories, scars, regrets, uncountable deaths, and losses we as a people and country have sustained are unforgettable. Our imperfections and hatred toward each other can no longer live amongst us if we must peacefully coexist to develop a perfect society where all of us can live once again as Liberians.

Let us be reminded that though the physical displacements or movements of people internally and externally may have ended or subsided, though some levels of the normalcy of life are returning to Liberia, we cannot stop walking mentally as though the past is gone and cannot be repeated, as has become the way of thinking of some Liberians. We must mentally engage our past and continuously focus on the ideals needed to bring about social and societal change. Failure to do so is a recipe for the reoccurrence of the same mistakes that brought us to this period in our history.

It cannot be said louder or clearer than this; we have come too far in our history, one hundred and seventy-four years of existence, and we cannot

---

3. "Meaning of 'Zion Train.'"

look back now. We have made enormous sacrifices to come this far. Those who came before us suffered and bled so that we could have the freedom and country we enjoy today. They have deposited a huge sum of money into our bank accounts, but the accounts are beginning to run low on funds. It is our time to replenish the funds so that our children and grandchildren may have enough money to spend and cultivate the audacity to do likewise. We must muster the courage to face the giant, which has left Liberia further behind other nations, especially in Africa.

Winston Churchill once said, "Fear is a reaction, and courage is a decision."[4] We must not allow the fear of the unknown nor the courage of thinking and undertaking great adventures to frighten or overwhelm us. We must seek any idea, cause, investment, or education that would give us the authority to make our presence felt on the "Zion Train" of social and societal change.

We must not allow ourselves to be held back or prevented from joining those who seek social and societal change to our way of life and in Liberia. We must embrace forward march as our drill order. We must plot the course of change needed in our society so desperately to save our republic. We must not fear to confront the truth or fail to expose the ills within our society that have driven us so deep into the darkness of underdevelopment, unproductivity, division, nepotism, tribalism, sectionalism, and a lack of nationalism.

We must lawfully confront and reject those who seek to exploit and divide us, our children, and resources with their misleading philosophies and ideologies. Now is the time for us to pick up from where our ancestors brought us so that our children may have the opportunity to pick up from where we take them. We must preserve a future and a country for our children that they can be proud of and call home. The argument posits that a divided nation is prone to embrace the culture of perpetual violence and anarchy within its fold. This phenomenon is aligned or synonymous with Achebe's ideology that "when things fall apart, the Centerpiece cannot hold."[5]

We do not have to do more than we can to bring about social and societal change. It starts with us by doing the little we can do in good faith and our country's interest. The little we can do—for example, having dialogues amongst ourselves about social and societal change, writing about it for others to read and take actions, investing in Liberia, speaking with our elected officials about the change we expect, praying for our leaders,

---

4. Langworth, "All the 'Quotes' Churchill Never Said."
5. Gbote and Kgatla, "Role of Christianity."

training our children, sending them to school to prepare them for tomorrow and help our youth who bore the most burden of the civil crisis to become better citizens. This will have a greater impact in our society than we can think or imagine.

We can't stop walking unless we have done what is required of each of us. We can't stop walking unless we pay our dues to replenish the amounts deposited in our bank accounts by our ancestors. We are indebted to them, our children, and our generation. We cannot escape making good on our payments, or else the accounts will be closed. History will judge us if we fail to do our individual and collective parts to maintain this sacred and ancestral ritual. We must not allow this to happen in our time. Therefore, we must continue to walk mentally in one direction and with one purpose until we achieve a true spirit of nationalism.

APPENDIX

Glossary of Traditional Liberian Names and Meanings

NAMES OF CITIES, TOWNS, AND FOOD ITEMS

Bahn's Town—*a local town in Kokoyah District.*

Bamboo bench—*locally made bench from bamboo trees.*

Bamboo mat—*a sleeping bed made from a bamboo tree. It also has other uses.*

Bamboo tree—*bamboos are a group of woody perennial evergreen plants in the true grass family Poaceae. It is used by locals to make furniture and furniture-like items.*

Bamboo wine/Palm wine—*locally produced alcoholic beverages made from palm or bamboo trees and sold in the local markets. The locals, especially men, usually consume them.*

Bassa tribe—*once known as "people of the forest." Good hunters of animals and gatherers of fruits and vegetables. Live in Grand Bassa County—Southeastern Liberia.*

Bitter balls—*tropical vegetables.*

Blemie—*a gold mining town in Nimba County, Liberia.*

Boduala ("bo-dua-la")—*a remote village across the St. Paul River in lower Bong County*

Appendix

Bong County—one of several counties located in the north-central area of Liberia.

Bong Mines—an iron ore mining community located in Bong County, central Liberia.

Boom-bor ("bomb-bor")—a locally made short pant constructed from pieces of cloths, usually worn by boys and girls in the interior areas of Liberia.

Botota—the headquarters of Kokoyah District.

Cassava—a starchy root vegetable. It comes from the underground tuberous root of the Cassava shurub, which is cultivated in South America, Africa, and Southeast Asia.

Conga drum—a tall, narrow, single-headed drum from cuba, also known as a "tumbadora." There are three types of conga: quinto, tres dos or tres golpes, and tumba or salidor.

Dean's Town—a gold mining town in Kokoyah not far from Saye Wheh Town.

Djembe drums—a djembe or jembe is a rope-tuned, skin-covered goblet drum played with bare hands, originally from West Africa. "Dje" means gather and "be" means everyone, which gave the drum used in these calls to order its name.

Freedom fighter—a person who takes part in a violent struggle to achieve a political goal, especially to overthrow their government.

Fufu—a dough made from boiled and pounded starchy ground provisions like plantains, cassava, or malanga.

Galamsey—small-scale illegal gold miners.

Ganta—originally "Garpa" or "Gumpa," but was changed by tax collectors from the Kpelle ethnic group, who added "ta" to "Gan," resulting in "Ganta," with "ta" meaning town.

Garri—a dry cream-white flour mainly consumed in West Africa. It is obtained by processing the starchy tuberous root of freshly harvested cassava in a sequence of demanding steps involving peeling, washing, crushing, fermenting, drying, and frying.

Gbarnga—on the farm (some believe it means a small pile of dead branches or wood).

Gbecon ("gbe-con")—a local town in Kokoyah District where Kerkula sought treatment.

Gbetu ("gbe-tu")—aka Country Devil, a traditional name given to a specific societal personality. A helmet mask with a raffia costume is a men's

Glossary of Traditional Liberian Names and Meanings

masquerade performed primarily for secular entertainment. Mainly found in the Gola tribe in Liberia.

Gboanipea—*a goal mining town in Nimba County, Liberia.*

Gbohn's Town—*a small town in Kokoyah District, Bong County.*

Gboweh ("gbo-weh")—*the name of a mourning dove.*

General "Mosquito"—*a strong fighter of the NPFL.*

Gio tribe—*tribal group in northeastern Liberia and the Ivory Coast. They are from Nimba County.*

Grand Cape Mount County—*one of five original counties in the northwestern portion of Liberia.*

Kakata—*"Kaka" is a name of a person and "ta" means town.*

Kehyoo ("keh-yoo")—*a warning sign which alerts villagers who are non-members of the tribal society to go into hiding due to the arrival of Gbetu, the "Country Devil."*

Kerkula—*a traditional Kpelle name.*

Kokoyah ("klo-klo-ya")—*meaning a solid or firm object or substance; a district in upper Bong County mostly inhabited by the Kpelle, Mano, Gio, and predominately Bassa tribes.*

Kpelle tribe—*the largest ethnic group in Liberia. They are from Bong County.*

Loguatuo—*a town on a hill called Logua.*

Mandingo—*mostly Muslims who engage in trade and commerce. Found relatively in all counties in Liberia but predominantly in Nimba County.*

Mano tribe—*mostly found in the northeastern part of Liberia in Nimba County. Excellent in art and craft and good musicians and farmers.*

Nimba—*aka "Nenbaa ton," means slippery mountain where beautiful young girls slip and fall.*

Nimba County—*located in the northeastern region of Liberia. Second largest (in population) and one of the original nine counties with the size of 4,650 square miles.*

Okra—*tropical vegetable.*

Palava hut—*a "meeting hut" or "hut for discussion." Derived from "palavra," a Portuguese word for discussion or meeting.*

Peppers—*tropical vegetables.*

Poro Society—a male secret society in Liberia responsible for initiating boys into manhood.

Rebel—a person who rises in opposition or armed resistance against an established government or ruler.

Sande Society—a female version of a secret society in Liberia that is responsible for initiating girls into womanhood.

"San-ga-lay-go-wa"—"you come against us and fail; we come against you and win."

Sanniquellie—originally Sein Gbein (a quarter named after "Sein"), but the name was changed by tax collectors from the Kpelle ethnic group, who added "quellie" to "Sanni."

Saye Wheh Town—town named after Mr. Saye Wheh, the founder of the village.

Single file—a line of people or things arranged one behind another.

St. Paul River—a major river in Liberia which rises in Guinea, West Africa, with its source northwest of the Nimba Range.

Tappita—one of six districts in Nimba County, Liberia.

Yeeli ("yea-la")—a small river in Kokoyah District where Kerkula and his friends met the "raft man."

Yolo's Town—a small village east of Saye Wheh Town.

Zorgowee—honey town; a town named after honeybees.

About the Author

MURPHY VATIKEH SIRLEAF ANDERSON is a believer in community organizations and an advocate of social justice, equality, human dignity, and freedom for all people. He is the current director of programs for the Association of Liberian Lutherans in the Americas (ALLIA). He is the former chairman of the boards of directors of ALLIA and Liberians in Columbus (LICI). Murphy has a graduate certificate in Public and Non-Public Leadership from The Ohio State University, an MBA from Capital University in Columbus, Ohio, an MSA from Central Michigan University (CMU), Mt. Pleasant, Michigan, and is a candidate for a Doctor of Health Administration (DHA) degree at CMU. He is a member of the National Black MBA Association, Amnesty International, the Liberian Studies Association (LSA), and a case manager with Franklin County Department of Job and Family Services, State of Ohio.

Other works by the author:

Bibliography

"African Names from Liberia West Africa." TLC African. https://www.tlcafrica.com/african_names_liberia.htm.

Anderson, Murphy V. S. *A Journey to Bong Mines*. Eugene, OR: Wipf & Stock, 2020.

Bahoo, S., et al. "Corruption in International Business: A Review and Research Agenda." *International Business Review* 29:4 (2019). https://doi.org/10.1016/j.ibusrev.2019.101660.

Bayer, C. P., et al. "Association of Trauma and PTSD Symptoms with Openness to Reconciliation and Feelings of Revenge among Former Ugandan and Congolese Child Soldiers." *JAMA* 298:5 (2007) 555–59. PubMed: 17666676.

Bellamy, Carol. "Children Are War's Greatest Victims." *OECD Observer*, May 22, 2002. https://oecdobserver.org/news/archivestory.php/aid/701/Children_are_war_s_greatest_victims.html.

Betancourt, T. S., et al. "Sierra Leone's Former Child Soldiers: A Follow-Up Study of Psychosocial Adjustment and Community Reintegration." *National Institute of Health* 81:4 (2010) 1077–95.

Brussat, Frederic, and Mary Ann Brussat. Review of *The Seeker's Guide: Making Your Life a Spiritual Adventure*, by Elizabeth Lesser. Spirituality and Practice. https://www.spiritualityandpractice.com/books/reviews/view/1771.

Christensen, C. T. "The Effects of Trumpet Construction on Literature from Antiquity through the Classic Period." *Undergraduate Research Journal* 20:5 (2016) 555–59.

Case, L. "An Ode to the Single-Shot Shotgun." *American Hunter*, June 19, 2018. https://www.americanhunter.org/articles/2018/6/19/an-ode-to-the-single-shot-shotgun/.

"Children, Not Soldiers." UN Office of the Special Representative of the Secretary-General for Children and Armed Conflict, 2014. https://childrenandarmedconflict.un.org/children-not-soldiers/.

"Combating Corruption." World Bank, 2018. Retrieved April 20, 2020, updated regularly. https://www.worldbank.org/en/topic/governance/brief/anti-corruption.

"Definition of a Christian." Focus on the Family. https://www.focusonthefamily.com/family-qa/definition-of-a-christian/.

"Dozens Missing and Feared Dead after Liberia Gold Mine Collapse." *Aljazeera*, May 6, 2020. https://www.aljazeera.com/news/2020/05/dozens-missing-feared-dead-liberia-gold-collapse-200506072134858.html.

Dunbar, Alline. "Liberia: More4Education Coalition Expresses Dismay over the Low Education Budget." *FrontPage Africa*, Jan 17, 2020. https://frontpageafricaonline.com/news/liberia-more4education-coalition-expresses-dismay-over-low-education-budget/.

Dunton, Genevieve F., and Margaret Schneider. "Perceived Barriers to Walking for Physical Activity." *Preventing Chronic Disease* 3:4 (2006) 127–29. http://www.cdc.gov/pcd/issues/2006/oct/05_0185.htm.

Doloquee, F. "Breaking News: Liberia: Over 40 Illegal Miners Buried Underground." *FrontPage Africa*, July 11, 2020. https://frontpageafricaonline.com/front-slider/breaking-news-liberia-over-40-illegal-miners-buried-underground/.

Eckersley, Richard M. "Culture, Spirituality, Religion and Health: Looking at the Big Picture." *Medical Journal of Australia* 186:10 (2007) S54.

Efrizah, Doni. "Supernatural Power in William Shakespeare's The Tempest." First Annual International Conference on Language and Literature. *KnE Social Sciences* 3:4 (2018) 266–77. Doi: 10.18502/kss.v3i4.1938.

Emmanuel, Aboka Y., et al. "Review of Environmental and Health Impacts of Mining in Ghana." *Journal of Health and Population* 8:17 (2018) 43–52.

Erwin, M. W. "The Powers: 12 Principles to Transform Your Life from Ordinary to Extraordinary." New York: Skyhorse, 2016.

Fernsby, Christian. "62 Arrested for Illegal Mining in Ghana." *Post Online Media*, December 15, 2019. https://www.poandpo.com/news/62-arrested-for-illegal-mining-in-ghana-15122019602/.

Field, H. "Biographical Sketches of Hitler and Himmler." Office of strategic services, 1943. https://www.cia.gov/library/readingroom/docs/HITLER%2C%20ADOLF_0001.pdf.

"Galamsey." *Oxford Advanced Learner's Dictionary*. https://www.oxfordlearnersdictionaries.com/us/definition/english/.

Galland, Olivier, and Yannick Lemel. "Tradition vs. Modernity: The Continuing Dichotomy of Values in European Societies." *Revue française de sociologie* 49:5 (2008) 153–86.

"Gari." African Foods: Bringing Africa Home, 2005. https://www.africanfoods.co.uk/gari.html.

Gbote, Eric Z. M., and Selaelo T. Kgatla. "Prosperity Gospel: A Missiological Assessment." *HTS Teologiese Studies* 70:1 (2014) 1–10. https://doi.org/10.4102/hts.v70i1.2105.

———. "The Role of Christianity in Mending Societal Fragility and Quelling Violence in Liberia." *Verbum et Ecclesia* 38:1 (2017) 1–10. https://verbumetecclesia.org.za/index.php/VE/article/view/1651.

Gould, Skye, and Jenny Cheng. "Wise Quotes on Life, Liberty, and the Pursuit of Happiness from Every US President." Business Insider, February 18, 2019. https://www.businessinsider.com/inspirational-quotes-from-us-presidents-2017-2.

Hanson, Sarah, and Andy Jones. "Is There Evidence That Walking Groups Have Health Benefits? A Systematic Review and Meta-Analysis." *British Journal of Sports Medicine* 49:11 (2015) 710–15.

Harris, Ed. "The Single 12 Gauge Shotgun." 2014. https://www.hensleygibbs.com/edharris/articles/Single-Barrel_Shotgun.htm.

"Helmet Mask (Gbetu) with Raffia Costume." Brooklyn Museum, 2020. https://www.brooklynmuseum.org/opencollection/objects/198928.

Hill, Napoleon. *Think and Grow Rich*. Meriden, CT: Ralston Society, 1937.

Hoff, Samuel B. "Commentary: Presidential Quotes on War, Memorial Day and Sacrifice." *Delaware State News*, May 27, 2018.

Bibliography

"Iosif Vissarionovich Dzhugashvili / Joseph Stalin (1879–1953)." *Global Security*, last modified April 20, 2019. https://www.globalsecurity.org/military/world/russia/stalin.htm.

Javaid, Aliraza. "The Sociology and Social Science of 'Evil': Is the Conception of Pedophilia Evil?" *Philosophical Papers and Review* 6:1 (2015) 1–9.

Jeremiah, David. *Everything You Need: 8 Essential Steps to a Life of Confidence in the Promises of God*. Nashville: Thomas Nelson, 2019.

———. "What Is Godliness?" *David Jeremiah Blog*. https://davidjeremiah.blog/what-is-godliness/.

Kohrt, Brandon. "Recommendations to Promote Children's Psychosocial Well-Being Associated with Armed Forces and Armed Groups (CAAFAG) in Nepal." UNICEF, 2007.

Kaufmann, Daniel, and Aart Kraay. "Governance Indicators: Where Are We, Where Should We Be Going?" *Policy Research Working Papers*, WPS4370. https://info.worldbank.org/governance/wgi/pdf/wps4370.pdf.

Kaufmann, Daniel, et al. "The World Governance Indicators: Methodology and Analytical Issues." *Policy Research Working Papers* 2010, WPS5430. http://info.worldbank.org/governance/wgi/pdf/wgi.pdf.

Langworth, Richard M. "All the 'Quotes' Churchill Never Said (2: Fanatic to Liberty)." November 16, 2018. https://richardlangworth.com/quotes-churchill-never-said-2.

Lee-Jones, Krista, et al. "Liberia: Overview of Corruption and Anti-corruption." *Transparency International*, September 7, 2019.

Lesser, Elizabeth. "Fearlessness." *Our Inner Lives*. https://www.feminist.com/ourinnerlives/inspiration_lesser4.html.

"Liberia." UNESCO, 2017. http://uis.unesco.org/en/country/lr?theme=education-and-literacy.

Longman, Molly. "Cassava: The Ingredient You Are Seeing Everywhere, and You Should Know About." *Refinery29*, November 5, 2019. https://www.refinery29.com/en-us/what-is-cassava-yuca.

"Meaning of 'Zion Train' by Bob Marley." Song Meanings and Facts, September 6, 2018. https://www.songmeaningsandfacts.com/zion-train-by-bob-marley/.

Melgar, Natalia, et al. "The Perception of Corruption." *International Journal of Public Research* 22:1 (2010) 120–31. https://doi.org/10.1093/ijpor/edp058.

Miller, Jake C. "The Homeless of Africa." *Africa Today* 29:2 (1982) 5–30.

Morse, Felicity. "Who Said It: Joseph Stalin or Oliver Cromwell?" *Independent*, December 20, 2013. https://www.independent.co.uk/news/people/who-said-it-joseph-stalin-or-oliver-cromwell-9017590.html.

Nagaraj, A. K. M., et al. "The Mystery of Reincarnation." *Indian Journal of Psychiatry* 57:4 (2015) 439.

Norris, D. K. "More Statements on the Ebola Virus Disease." *Sites of Liberia*, 2014. https://sitesofliberia.wordpress.com/.

Nietzsche, Friedrich. *The Gay Science*. Edited by Walter Kaufman. New York: Vintage, 1974.

"2008 Population and Housing Census: Analytical Report on Population Size and Composition." Republic of Liberia, 2008. https://www.lisgis.net/pg_img/Population%20size%20210512.pdf.

Ozturk, Ilhan. "The Role of Education in Economic Development: A Theoretical Perspective." *Journal of Rural Development and Administration* 33:1 (2001) 39–47.

Okeke, Chukwuma O., et al. "Conflicts between African Traditional Religion and Christianity in Eastern Nigeria: The Igbo Example." *SAGE Open* (2017) 1–10. https://journals.sagepub.com/doi/pdf/10.1177/2158244017709322.

Parris, Matthew. "As an Atheist, I Truly Believe Africa Needs God." *The Times*, December 27, 2008. https://www.thetimes.co.uk/article/as-an-atheist-i-truly-believe-africa-needs-god-3xj9bm8oh8m.

Paye-Layleh, J. "Liberia Illicit Gold Mine Collapse: Five Bodies Found." *BBC News*, February 13, 2019. https://www.bbc.com/news/world-africa-47224917.

Petrus, T. S., and D. L. Bogopus. "Natural and Supernatural: Intersections between the Spiritual and Natural World in African Witchcraft and Healing with Reference to South Africa." *The Indo-Pacific Journal of Phenomenology* 7:1 (2007) 1–10.

Ratcliffe, Susan, ed. *Oxford Essential Quotations*. 4th ed. Oxford: Oxford University Press, 2016.

Rohrer, Finlo. "The Slow Death of Purposely Walking." *BBC News Magazine*, May 1, 2014. https://www.bbc.com/news/magazine-27186709.

Roosevelt, Theodore. *The Works of Theodore Roosevelt, Memoir Edition*. Volume XVII.

Stur, Heather. "Why the United States Went to War in Vietnam." *Foreign Policy Research Institute*, April 28, 2017. https://www.fpri.org/article/2017/04/united-states-went-war-vietnam/.

"Summative Evaluation of GPE's Country-Level Support to Education: Batch 2, Country 2—Liberia; Final Report." Global Partnership for Education, August 2018. https://www.globalpartnership.org/sites/default/files/2018-12-gpe-evaluation-report-liberia.pdf.

Sunnyway, Elton S. Interview by the author on Saye Wheh Town. May 30, 2020.

Taryor, N. K. *Liberia Facing Mount Nimba: A Documentary History of the United Nimba Citizens' Council (UNICCO)*. Chicago: Strugglers', 1991.

Tauber, Alan. "History of the Djembe." Drum Connection. https://www.drumconnection.com/africa-connections/history-of-the-djembe/.

Tzu, Sun. *The Art of War*. New York: Penguin, 2009.

Triebert, Christiaan. "Ghana's Atewa Forest: Monitoring Mining, Which May Threaten Water Sources." *Bellingcat*, August 14, 2017. https://www.bellingcat.com/news/africa/2017/08/14/mining-in-the-atewa-forest/.

"Violations against Children in Conflict Continue to Rise, Secretary-General Tells Security Council, Blaming 'Shameful Disregard for Civilian Lives.'" United Nations Press Release, February 20, 2020. https://www.un.org/press/en/2020/sgsm19971.doc.htm.

Wilson, Samuel T. K, et al. "The Mining Sector of Liberia: Current Practices and Environmental Challenges." *Environ Sci Pollut Res* 24 (2017) 18711–20. Doi: 10.1007/s11356-017-9647-4.

Wood, John C., and Michael C. Wood, eds. *George Elton Mayo Critical Evaluation in Business and Management*. Vol. 1. London: Routledge, 2004.

Zackpah, Augustine. Interview by the author on Saye Wheh Town. May 31, 2020.

Zacharias, Ravi. "East and West, Part 1." *Let My People Think* podcast, April 20, 2020. https://www.rzim.org/listen/let-my-people-think/east-and-west-part-1.

———. "Hebrew, Romans and Greeks—Light, Glory and Knowledge." *A Modern Puritan*, November 19, 2013. https://modernpuritan.com/category/men-women-of-the-faith/ravi-zacharias/.

———. "The Nihilistic Outcome." *Just a Thought* podcast, October 19, 2018. https://www.rzim.org/listen/just-a-thought/the-nihilistic-outcome.

———. "Uncovering the New Spirituality, Part 1." *Let My People Think* podcast, April 4, 2020. https://www.truthnetwork.com/show/let-my-people-think-ravi-zacharias/18385/.

———. "A Universal Madness." *Just a Thought* podcast, July 21, 2017. https://www.rzim.org/listen/just-a-thought/a-universal-madness.

———. "Who Are You, God? Part 1 of 4." *Just Thinking* podcast, August 28, 2017. https://www.rzim.org/listen/just-thinking/who-are-you-god-part-1-of-4.

www.ingramcontent.com/pod-product-compliance
Lightning Source LLC
Chambersburg PA
CBHW070918160426
43193CB00011B/1514